THE
EMBROIDERER'S
COUNTRY
ALBUM

HELEN
STEVENS

THE
EMBROIDERER'S
COUNTRY
ALBUM

HELEN M. STEVENS

David & Charles

For Brian, with love and
thanks for quite a year!

Photography throughout by
Fotofayre, Bury St Edmunds, Suffolk

PLATE 1

◁ *PLATE 1*

*Frontispiece. 'Four, it is the Dilly hour, when
blooms the Gilly flower'. The Dilly Song, or
the Keys of Heaven, is an ancient folk song
recalling the Embroidress's flower. Today, the
various hybrid wallflowers* (Cheiranthus)
*are a common sight in both town and
country gardens*
Embroidery shown life size:
20.5 x 25.5cm (8 x 10 inches)

A DAVID & CHARLES BOOK
Copyright text and illustrations © Helen M. Stevens 1994
Photography Copyright © David & Charles 1994
First published 1994

Helen M. Stevens has asserted her right to be identified as author of this work in accordance with the
Copyright, Designs and Patent Act 1988.

A catalogue record for this book is available from the British Library.

ISBN 0 7153 0207 8

Typeset by Greenshires Icon, Exeter, Devon
and printed in Italy by LEGO SpA, Vicenza
for David & Charles
Brunel House, Newton Abbot, Devon.

CONTENTS

HELEN
STEVENS

PREFACE

THE EMBROIDRESS'S TALE

According to a fourteenth-century folk tale, her father was the town tailor, her mother the seamstress, and Gilly-anne had inherited their skills with the needle. Her father's tailoring graced the best houses and her mother's dresses the finest salons, but Gilly-anne had no wish to use her needle for profit; rather, she loved to stroll the narrow country lanes and return to her room, where, with silks of a hundred bright colours, she would recreate the flowers she had collected on her rambles, bright daisies, nodding poppies, sky-blue cornflowers and tumbling masses of wild briar roses. She had one other love, a farmer's boy who walked with her, reaching up into the tall hedgerows to gather the blossoms beyond her grasp.

Her father became impatient, her mother critical. 'Time that girl earned a living', said one. 'A few days locked in her room will soon take the stars from her eyes', said the other, and so Gilly-anne found herself locked away with only her embroidery needle for company and a hundred bright silks. Each day her lover walked below her window, but try as he might he could not reach her hand, and as she leaned down to him, the only flowers they could share were the golden yellow wallflowers which clung to the wall of her prison. They resolved to elope.

Her embroidery hoop lay idle. Gilly-anne twisted the hundred bright silks into a rainbow coloured rope.

> Up she got upon the wall,   Love, in pity of the dead,
> Tempting down to slide withall,   And her loving luckless speed
> But the silken twist untied,   Turned her to this plant we call
> So she fell and bruised and died.   Now the flower of the wall.

(Robert Herrick, 1591–1674)

The country name for the wallflower is still the Gilly flower, the Embroidress's flower, once only golden yellow, but now of a hundred bright colours.

INTRODUCTION

*'As soon as you find you can do
anything, do something you can't.'
I worked with the material in three or
four overlaid tints and textures ... it
was like working with lacquer and mother-
o'-pearl ... and trying not to let the
joins show.*

Something of Myself
Rudyard Kipling

PLATE 4 △

*From miniatures to pressed flowers and real
butterflies, the Victorians knew no bounds in
their passion for collecting. In embroidery, we
can combine many aspects of creating the perfect
album without recourse to picking flowers or
asphyxiating insects! Complemented by a
miniature silver frame, this tiny study of
flowers and butterflies would be a jewel in any
collection. Techniques for 'miniaturizing'
subjects, mounting and framing are discussed
fully in later chapters*
6.5 x 8.5cm (2½ x 3¼ inches)
including frame

. . . .

B y the late Victorian era, the art of creating the perfect album had reached its
zenith. The passion for collecting, love of arranging those collections
attractively, and enthusiasm for learning through the study of odds and ends of
information and material gathered during travel or the enjoyment of everyday life,
matured into the ability to put together diaries, journals, folios and albums which
to modern eyes are incredible feats of patience and inspiration.

By its very nature, an album is eclectic. Like a patchwork quilt in book form
it can bring together snippets recalling a favourite memory, the snapshot of an old
friend, the sketch of a family home now long gone, scraps, recipes and designs.
Embroidery, too, is an eclectic art. For generations techniques have been passed
on, elaborated, absorbed and reborn, each embroiderer selecting the effects which
best suited the subject matter and using designs which in times past might have
originated in woodcuts and rough prints, but which today we derive from an
enormous variety of media, ranging from high-tech video to studies of Victorian
collections of flora, fauna and country life.

The choice is ours: a 'Country Album' will naturally contain trees and
flowers, birds and butterflies, churches, fields, barns and cottages, but these alone
form only part of the story of the *Embroiderer's Country Album*.

Mankind has always sought to change the environment and, for better or for
worse, has succeeded in altering almost every aspect of the natural world.
At worst, this has resulted in the destruction of many plants and animals, but in
other instances, where change has come slowly, our interdependence with nature

◁ *PLATE 5*
*'Rectory Cottage'. The use of detail and
contrasting directional stitching immediately
begins to put life into even a small landscape
embroidery. The same techniques may be used
to create a broad, sweeping canvas*
9.5 x 8.0cm (3¾ x 3 inches)

has created new habitats, beautiful and successful harmonies of wild and cultivated land and protected places where creatures once threatened by man can thrive in safety.

Since man first clothed himself and insulated and decorated his home, the need for textiles has played an important part in the changing face of the countryside. Raw materials for woven and plied fabrics, dye-stuffs, spinning, carding and other manufacturing necessities were first gathered from the wild and later cultivated as demand outstripped the supply of naturally occurring crops. The wide, timber-fronted streets of many villages owe their attractive appearance to the frequent passing, generations ago, of huge flocks of sheep bound for market; some towns even owe their names to the textile trade: Saffron Walden in Essex still conjures up a vision of wide acres of golden flowers, the raw dye for many a fine fabric.

What better medium, then, to explore this heritage than embroidery? Of course, the most obvious contribution man has made towards what we now consider to be the countryside is his building, but how is it

Fig 1 ▷
*Many countryside flowers still bear witness to
the importance of the textile industry in earlier
generations. Flax, madder and the meadow
saffron still commonly grow in areas where
they were once cultivated*

Fig 2 ▷
*A rough sketch may include distance and
foreground features wildly entangled – what it
means to you is all important. The rough
texture of old bark stripping from dead
branches, the springy resilience of meadow
grasses, the gentle undulation of a hilly
landscape all serve to capture the atmosphere
of a scene*

PLATE 6 ▷
*As man gradually tamed his environment,
wild oats* (Avena fatua) *gave way to
cultivated varieties, and the wood mouse*
(Apodemus sylvaticus) *became less welcome
to his share. The rigid, spiky hairs on the oats,
the short grasses and the whiskers on the mouse
are in sharp contrast to the smoothness of the
fur and soft, rounded stitching on the daisy
and its leaves. In close up, contrast stitching
is still important*
11.5 x 17.25cm (4½ x 6¾ inches)
. . . .

possible to capture the solid charm of an eighteenth-century cottage, a Norman church, a winding village street in a tactile, fluid medium? The answer is two-fold: by the use of contrast and detail, principles which form the basis of much of the landscape and architectural embroidery in this book.

A finished work of landscape embroidery should appeal on two levels: first, as a complete picture, to be viewed as a whole, and second, inviting closer inspection of its individual component parts. Broadly speaking, the contrast of large and small stitches build up the overall effect, while the minutiae are effected by a gradual build-up of impressionistic touches. In *The Embroiderer's Countryside* I explored ways in which it was possible to create lifelike studies of nature in close up – and these techniques will form the basis of most foregrounds in this book (there is a summary of the most basic techniques in Appendix A). Now it will be possible to penetrate deeper into those countryside scenes, and, by the use of new techniques, convey not only nature itself, but also man's interaction with his

environment – his buildings, the altered landscapes of fen and farmland and the introduction of new species, trees, shrubs and herbs.

There is also, of course, much still be to be explored in close up. Nature's inspiration is inexhaustible and new combinations of subject matter lead the embroiderer on to more and more stimulating ideas. The whiskery fieldmouse and equally bewhiskered ears of wild oats (Plate 6); the comical starling, so commonplace and yet with the sunlight catching his iridescent feathers so spectacular; the warty toad, the texture of his skin so entirely different to almost any other creature's – all these can be captured through the different use of silks and cottons. Working the *underside* of a butterfly's wing is very different from working the top: the more minutely nature is uncovered, the more challenges she presents.

Despite the many sources available to us for research, there is still no substitute for the notebook and sketchpad. Few of us are able spontaneously to dash off a perfect study of a wildflower, tree or building – let alone capture the fleeting moment of a bird in flight. Yet, however basic a sketch may be, it serves as an important *personal* reminder of a scene (Fig 2). A cottage nestling upon the bank of a river, the broad sweep of lawn leading to a stately home, half-buried pebbles on a beach – even if a jotting captures only the roughest positioning of the elements it can be taken back to the drawing board and used as the basis for a more detailed design. Remember that the written word can be a help too. 'Bright sunlight', 'mossy texture', 'wicked spines': a note made on the point of observation can be a great stimulus. For landscape and architectural embroidery,

Fig 3 ▷

The robin has been a welcome companion in the garden since time immemorial – look out for unusual combinations of subject matter. Why picture him on the garden spade like everyone else when a vegetable marrow makes a more interesting study?

◁ *PLATE 7*
Fortunately, many species of insect and flower still flourish in our 're-fashioned' countryside. Flowers such as the humble bindweed (Convolvulus arvensis) *flower alongside its spectacular cousin, the morning glory (cover picture and Plate 49). The bumble bee has its domestic counterpart and in many farming regimes it is now recognized that by encouraging ladybirds to control aphids, systemic insecticides can be withdrawn. A small study like this of common, everyday insects is an important record of how the countryside appears in the late twentieth century*
9.0 x 10.5cm (3½ x 4 inches)

photography, too, can play a part, but it is important to remember that what 'works' as a photograph may well not translate satisfactorily into embroidery. Photography may be used as an *aide mémoire* in the same way as a rough sketch, but it should not be slavishly copied.

The countryside is constantly changing. The virgin forests and native woodland which covered most of Europe before man's advent have all but disappeared. They are to be mourned, but without their passing the countryside as we know and love it today could never have come into being. Where man's first roads crossed rivers small settlements sprang up, some are still villages, others have grown into great cities. Whole ecosystems have been created by man – not always consciously – such as the Fens and the Broads, and many species of plant, animal and bird now live in such close association with us that it is hard to imagine their lifestyles before the partnership was forged. (Where *did* swallows perch before there were telegraph wires?) We know, too, that damage has been done. Whereas the medieval embroiderer was able to include the wild boar and wolf as common animals of the English landscape, we cannot. We can only hope that the stag and the osprey do not follow their fate.

Embroidery has always enjoyed a role of social documentary. We must keep our eyes open for change. In the last decades of twentieth-century Britain one of

PLATE 8 ▷

'The Greening of Parliament'. Commissioned in 1990 and now hanging at Westminster, this embroidery illustrates perfectly how symbolism (the floral emblems of the United Kingdom), reality in the foreground and impressionism as the picture recedes can combine to create a satisfying whole. The formal addition of the portcullis devices serves to frame the main content. A clever camera angle when planning the picture obscured the worst of London's traffic, and small features such as the tiny figures to the left help direct the eye 39.5 x 46.0cm (15½ x 18 inches)

Fig 4 ▽

How personal your album becomes is up to you – my studio has been awaiting translation into embroidery for some time – so far only the sketch has been prepared!

the foremost innovations in country life is the barn conversion. Along with chocolate-box cottages and unconverted barns, surely it, too, should be recorded. Where ancient abbeys once stood, seemingly inviolable, now only ruins remain, their craggy weatherbeaten stones challenging our ingenuity. No album would be complete without rising to that challenge.

Even in the heart of the city, we need not feel frustrated in the search for suitable landscapes. In *The Embroiderer's Countryside*, small oases of the natural world in miniature were found on railway embankments and in cemeteries and gardens. To create a broader canvas, many buildings in urban areas can be found nestling among trees, subtly shaded by creepers and climbing plants, or softened by a plant-filled courtyard. While the roar of London traffic went on undimmed it was possible to capture the Palace of Westminster at an angle which made it appear a great cathedral of tranquillity, cars and buses obscured by planting, its massive sand-blasted façade complemented by the trees in Palace Green (Plate 8).

Embroidery is such a personal art form that, whatever suggestions are made, whatever innovations put forward, it is inevitable that they will be taken and used differently by each artist – and this is as it should be. The collection of embroideries put together in *this* album is indeed as personal and diverse as the snippets of fabric making up a patchwork quilt. I have tried to describe my techniques and my inspiration in such a way that they may be of help to other embroiderers. I hope that the by-roads and backwaters which have been explored along the way will appeal to country lovers, artists and embroiderers alike.

HELEN
STEVENS

CHAPTER ONE

THE EMBROIDERER'S VILLAGE

*'Why do you ever come back . . . what do you find
to attract you in this little country?'
'The call of lush meadow-grass, wet orchards, warm,
insect-haunted ponds, of browsing cattle, of hay-
making and all the farm buildings clustering
round the house . . .' replied the first swallow.*

The Wind in the Willows
Kenneth Grahame

A DESIRABLE RESIDENCE

Where and what is the embroiderer's village? To the historian it may be the fen settlement where a Saxon noblewoman gave up her fortune, dedicating her life to making embroideries for the great abbey at nearby Ely. To the romantic it may be that village you drove through once, long ago, an idyllic place of hollyhocks, quiet back lanes and cream teas – where inspiration struck, but never quite came to fruition. To others it may just be an impression, a dream of hot lazy summer afternoons, warm red brick walls and flaxen thatches.

Plate 9 captures a swallow's eye view of the approach to a typical country village. Nestling among folds of hilly arable land, a fourteenth-century church stands alongside a thatched cottage dating from the 1700s, its garden enclosed by a fine Victorian decorative wall, and a metalled road leading off to the village centre. Villages rarely stand still – for all the traditional charm of romantic cottages, ancient churchyards and old-fashioned gardens, if a small community is to survive it must adapt and, with luck, the best of every era will remain to delight the eye of the visitor. If embroidery is to recreate the changing face of the countryside, its villages, farmland and other man-made features – it too must be

◁ *PLATE 9*

The disappearance of the swallows (Hirundo rustica) *each autumn was once thought to be evidence that they buried themselves in the mud of rivers and ponds to await the coming of spring. Now we know that they migrate to the warmth of South Africa. They rarely alight on the ground, feeding and even drinking on the wing, and it is in flight that their spectacular form and colour can be captured to best advantage. The smooth, fuselage-shaped body, from striking russet throat patch to creamy underparts may be worked in radiating strata of* opus plumarium, *and whilst the feathering of the streamlined tail and wings may be treated similarly on inner regions (close to the body) primary feathers must be worked individually, as the filaments of each feather radiate from its central vein. All these characteristics, included in detail on the foreground bird, have also been incorporated in the working of the swallow shown in the distance.* Embroidery shown life size: 22.5 x 24cm (8¾ x 9½ inches)

◁ *PLATE 10*

The red admiral (Vanessa atalanta), *common in gardens, is an equally familiar sight in hedgerows and non-cultivated land. The Cheddar pink, which relies upon butterflies and moths for pollination, is by contrast becoming increasingly rare, and is now a protected plant. Its large, tufted flowers have the serrated petals typical of the* Dianthus *genus, which must be treated delicately in embroidery, each 'tooth' shadowed lightly by a fine stitch, the deep throat of the flower shot through with pale green.* 8.25 x 10.5cm (3¼ x 4 inches)

PLATE 11 ▷

*Cottage gardens well stocked with the finely
fragranced, densely headed sweet-william*
(Dianthus barbatus) *are the very essence of
'Olde England'. The Elizabethans grew many
varieties of pinks whose names survive as
charming witnesses to the fashions and fancies
of the day: 'Ruffling Robin', 'Master
Bradshawe and his Daintie Ladie' and, still
more evocatively, the 'Lustie Gallant'. In
happy contrast to the decline of many butterfly
species, the white admiral* (Ladoga camilla) *
has increased in numbers very considerably
since the eighteenth century, when it was
considered a rarity. This time, it is man's
neglect, rather than over-management of the
land, which has had the effect: the loss of
coppiced woodland with its tidy undergrowth
has in places allowed the rampant growth of
honeysuckle, the caterpillar's sole food-plant.
The dull appearance of the butterfly from above
is also excellent camouflage. The underside of a
butterfly's wing is altogether more matt than
the upper surface, and embroidery of the
pattern may therefore be achieved through the
use of shorter stitches of radial work, merging
less smoothly together. The veins, which are
very prominent, are overlaid by shooting
stitches taken outwards from the edge of the
inner strata towards the outside of the wing.
In this way they do not merge smoothly and are
realistically evident. The corona of pale stitches
on the outer fringes of the petals on the sweet-
william is worked similarly*
11 x 10.5cm (4¼ x 4 inches)

flexible and able to adapt design and technique to new challenges.

Radial stitching (see Appendix A, page 126) is the perfect medium for working the simple, open-faced flower of the Cheddar pink, the wild forerunner of many garden flowers from the carnation to the elaborate many headed sweet-william, just as basic techniques of *opus plumarium* (feather work, see page 127) are ideal for the butterfly's startlingly well-defined upper wing surfaces. But if we are to attempt more complicated, less obvious designs, it is necessary first to elaborate upon these techniques, before moving on to entirely new types of work.

While Plates 10 and 11 appear superficially to be very similar in concept, the differences between the two serve to throw into relief several important aspects of the work which is to be explored in later chapters, both in detailed studies and in broader 'landscape' embroideries. Plate 10 shows a conventional study of a red admiral approaching flowers. The species of butterfly has been chosen because it is not only attractive, but well known – a butterfly which most people find in their garden from time to time. Its wings are fully open, showing to best effect their striking red and black pattern, white and blue spots incorporated through the use of Dalmatian-dog technique (page 127). The flower heads, stems and leaves are, by contrast, simple (only in one place do the petals of the separate flowers overlap), and the perspective is achieved by placing the main body of the insect directly in front of the stems, between the eye of the viewer and the floral design.

Plate 11, on the other hand, shows a less obvious combination of butterfly and flower. The white admiral, seen from above is a rather dull, uninteresting muddy brown, its only wing pattern formed by white markings. From beneath, however, it is a delicate, ethereal creature of orange, gold and silver, shot through with lines and chevrons of black and white. Shown in flight, only one wing is completely in view, the other is seen at an angle as it approaches the sweet-william from the side, and it is the relative positioning of the two wings which in this case gives the perspective of the picture (see Fig 5). The sweet-william is a complex flower. Although each flower in itself is as simple as the head of the Cheddar pink, the petals are shot through with differing shades of pink, and cluster, overlapping each other, necessitating the use of outlining and voiding (page 126).

ANOTHER BRICK IN THE WALL

Perhaps the most obvious difference between landscapes which remain intact and virtually unchanged by man, and environments which have been bent to his will, is demarcation. As soon as land is carved up into parcels and possessions it is natural that the owner wishes to place some form of boundary between his property and the next. Arable fields and pastures divided by hedgerows have their natural counterparts in villages and towns in the shape of ornamental hedges and walls. Initially, shrubs used were taken from the wild, one of the first being the privet. The native privet *(Ligustrum vulgare)*, can still be found growing in the wild and does not prove to be a very satisfactory modern hedging plant as it loses its leaves in the winter, although in Elizabethan times it was widely used and was known as the 'prim' or 'primprint', a reference to those who felt it necessary to hide behind it. In the 1840s the oval-leaved privet was introduced from Japan, a semi-evergreen, now the staple hedging shrub of the British suburbs.

The privet creates an attractive motif in embroidery, especially thrown into relief against a black background, its tiny, star-like white flowers highlighted by touches of gold thread at the core of each four-petalled floret. They are easily recreated by the use of straight stitches radiating from individual cores, gold seed stitches worked either randomly at the centre of each core, or delicately radiating outwards where a floret reflexes, such as at the very top of the design in Plate 12. Leaves are worked by radiating stitches from the elongated core formed by their veins.

A typical village shrub such as the native privet attracts insects which would normally stay well outside man's domain unless tempted by a natural food source. The privet hawk moth, with its magnificent wingspan of 11.5cm (4½ inches), is one visitor which may well be seen at dusk, taking nectar from the flowers of the privet. The smooth, mossy texture of a moth's wing is an ideal subject upon which to practise radial *opus plumarium*, as the spots of a butterfly's wing (which necessitate Dalmatian-dog technique) tend to be replaced on a moth by

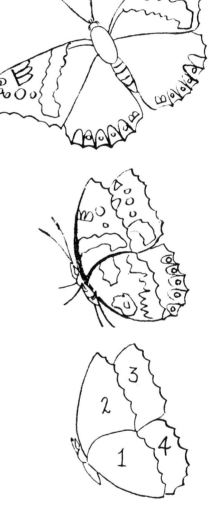

Fig 5 △

Worked in the open position the wing structure may be created in any symmetrical order, but seen in flight at an angle it is important to work the wings of butterflies in the order indicated, ie, the closest wing first (near bottom) then near top, far top and far bottom

PLATE 12a ▷
'Privet Cottage'. Staple hedging shrub of the suburbs, the privet has come to represent all the security of home. A simple, stylized study of a sturdy little house can be given a three-dimensional quality by careful attention to light and shadow. The trimmed, well-tended hedge surrounds the postage-stamp front garden and is worked entirely in seed stitching, lighter above and darker to the front and insides 7.5 x 10.25cm (3 x 4 inches)

graduated, merging strata. Its body, less obviously segmented than a butterfly's, can be conveyed through laddering (Appendix A, page 127), weaving a threaded needle through flat stitching already laid down.

The lilac, also shown in Plate 12, is not native to Britain, but has naturalized itself in many country hedgerows, having spread from gardens. It is often grafted on to the root stock of the common privet, and found growing in close proximity. It is unusual to see the flowers of the privet (usually in evidence in early July) open alongside the lilac (which blooms in May), but uncultivated shrubs can flower erratically, and it was a pretty enough combination to justify an entry in my notebook – a sketchpad not being to hand! *Contrast rounded florets of lilac with sharp petals of privet. Leaves on both shrubs opposite and undivided – reminiscent of Jacob's ladder.* Back to the drawing board, and a little judicious reference to textbooks allowed the preparation of the design. For a relatively simple study such as this, a note is often sufficient, but to begin to capture more complex shapes and textures, the sketchpad is invaluable – Plate 13 is typical.

The summer sun had warmed the old red-brick wall. In places it crumbled, wafer-thin slices falling away at a touch, green, yellow and gold lichens clinging to

HELEN
STEVENS

◁ *PLATE 12b*

Working on black, certain striking elements of a design which might otherwise not be seen to their greatest advantage, can be emphasized. One of the features which appealed to me in the creation of this study was the battling upward thrust of both shrubs as they contended with each other for light and space. Their leaves grew in the same arrangement, symmetrically placed (hence my allusion to the herb Jacob's ladder in my notebook, its regimented leaves like the rungs of a ladder), and there was a curious rhythmic surge which I echoed by including the privet hawk moth (Sphinx ligustri), its wings outstretched at the same angle as the flower heads. Unencumbered by the need for a shadow line, the delicate shades of the component parts of this study jump out of a dark canvas, whereas on a pale ground it might appear much less striking.

Impressionistic techniques work best on a lighter background, but where simplicity and boldness of line play an important part in a design it is always worth considering the use of a black fabric. Practical advice on fabrics may be found in Appendix B

11.5 x 16.5cm (4½ x 6½ inches)

Fig 6 ▷

Other hedging shrubs taken from the wild include the box (top left), hawthorn (top right) and blackthorn. Blackthorn flowers early, the leaves opening later, and in the autumn produces bitter sloes

PLATE 13 *(opposite)*

The clematis shown here is Clematis viticella, *not one of the new hybrid varieties of which there are so many, but an ancient and distinct species, which was known to medieval herbalists as the great bush bower. It was first brought to England in about 1569 and remains a cottage garden favourite, clinging tenaciously to walls, old trees, arbours and trellises. Like the truly wild, native* Clematis vitalba *(Plate 24) the flowers have no true petals, being formed by large colourful sepals which radiate from a thick mass of stamens.*

These, when the sepals fall, grow to considerable size, becoming feathered and fluffy – though not to the extent of the vitalba's *'hedge feathers'. The flowers are silvery underneath and a good subject on which to practise 'opposite angle' stitching (page 127). The mason bee (Osmia rufa) is similar to the honey bee in shape, and the sight of females busily squeezing into existing holes in walls and other brickwork has often led the uninitiated to fear that a swarm of wild bees may be forming. The egg hatches in about 14 weeks, and the young bee then remains cocooned through the winter. The bees' wings are worked in a very fine thread, superimposed by a strand of cellophane removed from a blending filament, both simply applied in long straight stitches 15.5 x 16.5cm (6 x 6½ inches)*

Fig 7 ▷

Create your own shorthand to note down textures and shadows. If you are familiar with the leaves of a climbing plant, these can be omitted for the time being while you concentrate upon the structure of the wall itself

its grainy surface. Where the partly discoloured mortar had flaked, mason bees widened the gaps, forcing their way into the body of the wall, sheltered by the clematis, its papery petals dark inside and silvered on their reverse.

While the species of bee and clematis might well be found in a good textbook, it would be impossible to find the atmospheric warmth of that wall, the oddly shaped circles and semi-circles of lichen. A sketch, however rough, must be

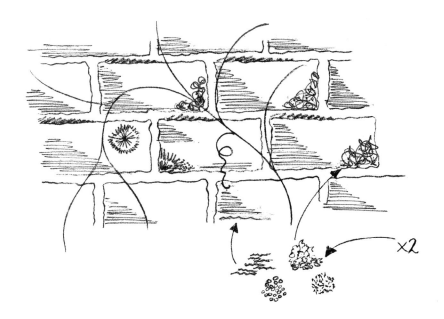

PLATE 14 ▷
Detail of Plate 1. Use your imagination to
recreate variations in texture in stonework,
moss and lichens. Seen in close up, the
individual stitches are evident, but from a little
distance the straight stitches in wool and silk,
and the surface couched, textured threads
merge into a satisfying whole
Dimensions of detail shown:
13 x 9cm (5 x 3½ inches)

made (Fig 7). Here we find the first key to noting and subsequently recreating the essential differences between embroidery of living, growing subjects and hard, immobile ones. Often, a few fluid lines are enough to convey the sweep of a leaf or stem, but more trouble must be taken with hard-baked bricks!

Try to establish your own form of shorthand – stubby dots for the grainy, unbroken surface of a brick; scratchy 'sunbursts' to locate lichens; a wavy line to show where one shade of colour merges into the next. It is not necessary to be a great artist – just a good observer. What appears in your sketchpad should make sense to *you*, not necessarily anyone else.

The same personal symbols which you have incorporated in your sketch (minus, of course, arrows, exclamation marks and written notes!) may be transferred on to your fabric ready to begin embroidery (see Appendix B). The flower leaves and buds should present no problems – they are simple matters of radial, stem and straight stitching – and should be worked first, as should the bees. The body of the bricks, the mortar, the lichens can then be built up around them, with contrast as the watchword. Where the flowers and leaves are smooth and glossy, the background must appear dull, grainy and solid. If floss silk has been used on the natural subjects, now is the time to experiment with twisted or plied silks (see Appendix B, Twisting Floss Silk). The brickwork in Plate 13 has been created by the use of stranded cotton and 4/1T silk. The stitches are very small and closely worked, although at random rather than in serried ranks, thus allowing either a smooth merging of colours, where variation in the shade of the brick is to be achieved, or a sharp cut-off such as between brick and mortar or mortar and lichen. This technique can be called dot stitching, finer than seed stitching, as each individual stitch should, at least from a short distance, appear to be spherical rather than even slightly elongated.

The lichens are created somewhat differently, depending on the particular properties of the individual. Green, mossy lichens are worked in bullion knots at the centre, French knots as they thin out toward their edge and dot stitching at their outermost limit, where they can merge into the brickwork. Flat, yellow lichens may be worked similarly at the core, and surrounded by a halo of straight radial stitching, and tiny green bodies of non-fruiting lichen by simple straight stitching.

By the use of all the techniques above, shown in various combinations in Plate 1 and its detail in Plate 14, it is possible to create in close up the hard surfaces of brick, stone, mortar and flint and contrast them with plants and insects in similar detail. How do we begin to use these principles in a more distant scene?

DOTS AND DASHES

Stroll down any village street and look about you. If you are confined to a city, try to find an avenue of houses and trees, or failing this, look up, above the shop fronts and traffic, to the windows above – often you will find window boxes, hanging baskets, even roof gardens softening the edges of the buildings. Even on the calmest of days there is some slight movement among the leaves, some liveliness of nature that sets it apart. Look beyond the movement to the building behind. That four-square solidity is what we have to capture.

Nature abhors a vacuum, it is said; it is also anathema to straight lines. When nature overruns a building, the first casualty is the rigid architectural precision of walls and roof. We delight in romantic ruins for this very reason. Immediately a truly straight line appears on the canvas, it is obvious that we are dealing with something man made. Living things, as we have discussed, have a glow of life about them – they are best worked in a floss thread. In the distance, just as in close up, bricks and mortar (or any building material) appear dull, and a twisted thread conveys this to better effect. The more jagged and uneven the surface to be recreated, the more matt it should appear.

Plate 15 shows in detail the techniques used to work the cottage and church at the opening of this chapter (Plate 9). There are three main building materials to be conveyed: flint, on the church; plasterwork on the cottage walls, and thatch. Just as shadowing is important in close-up natural studies (the shadow line is all important, see Appendix A, Outlining and voiding), so too it is necessary to indicate some light source in a broader study. The way in which this is conveyed may be called 'etching stitch' and forms the basis for the sturdiness of embroidered buildings. In close up, a single line of outline or stem stitch is

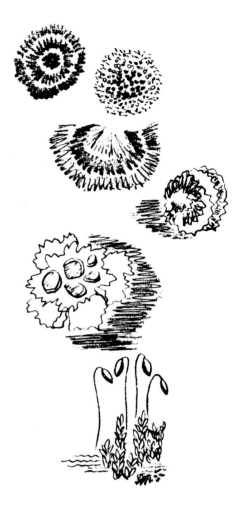

Fig 8 △
A close inspection of lichen and moss can be useful when you come to finalize your design. Try to note their direction of growth, and, where they stand proud from the wall, shadow beneath the main body to remind you of their three-dimensional qualities

. . . .

PLATE 15 △

Detail of Plate 9. The tree growing between the cottage and the church tower serves to separate the two and set the perspective between these principal features. By contrast, the ivy on the tower and the climbing roses on the wall of the cottage need to be shown as actually clinging to the surfaces of the buildings. Methods of achieving this differentiation will be discussed in later chapters. The cross on top of the tower is etched-in lightly in the finest possible thread

sufficient to indicate the shadow line – for landscape work more blocking of the shadow is needed: a large feature such as a church parapet or thatched gable end hangs over the feature beneath it creating a substantial shadow – this should be worked as a patch of perpendicular stitches (usually in black) beneath the overhanging feature. This etching should be worked first, just as a shadow line on a close up is the first step in creating the finished work, and when completed will give the effect of a 'pen and ink' sketch on your fabric.

Plate 15 shows an open, airy scene, the etching is fairly light, and around it one may now begin to build up the body of the buildings. From a distance, flintwork, so typical of East Anglian churches, appears a pock-marked jumble of colours, grey and brown, flecked with an occasional warm red – usually an old recycled brick. It can be effectively conveyed by the use of dot and seed stitching around, but not superimposed upon, the etching. Different storeys in the church tower are indicated by long straight horizontal stitches worked at the same time as the etching.

The cottage walls may be approached differently. They are basically smooth and devoid of features other than windows (to be discussed in later chapters) and the etched shadow of the eaves. Using a 2/1T cotton or silk they can be conveyed in long straight stitches covering the field of the motif – a similar technique may be used on the thatch (on this scale the details of individual features on the thatch itself are irrelevant – they will be explored in greater detail on a larger scale). These long, perpendicular stitches may be used to build up the body of the work, infilling the etching stitches on all types of architectural embroidery, from this simple cottage to the elaborate façades of more magnificent buildings, such as illustrated in Plate 8 and shown in detail in Plate 16. They should run only from one field of etching to the next, even where the etching itself is only one stitch deep. It is a quick, spontaneous type of stitching which we will call 'dashing' – in conjunction with the etching it *is* reminiscent of the dashed-off stroke of a pencil or crayon.

Etching, dotting and dashing will create the solid effect of buildings, but on their own these techniques, and the subjects they convey can be lifeless and dull. Contrast and 'movement' are needed to throw them into relief. In Plate 16 the towering hulk of the Victoria Tower (see full study on page 15) is softened by the trees and shrubs planted in the semi-foreground. They are placed directly between the eye and the main feature (just as the butterfly is placed between the viewer and the flower in Plate 10), and this perspective is created by bearing in mind the lie of the land in front of the building, ie, it is coming towards you and therefore appears *lower down* in your design.

This is a basic rule of perspective. 'I could never design my own embroideries – I'm terrified of drawing', is a statement often made by would-be creative embroiderers. Perspective, in particular, seems to be surrounded by an

◁ *Fig 9*
'Dashing' in embroidery creates a similar effect to the strokes of an artist's pencil. To practise etching and dashing try working a monochrome study in black and grey simply creating the form of the structure from its shadows

aura of mystery – but there are basically only two rules for the embroiderer to remember in landscape or architectural work. First: on the ground, the nearer a subject is the lower it appears. Second: whether at, above or below eye level, the nearer a subject is the larger it appears. This may sound elementary, but not until the Renaissance was this rule universally grasped by painters, and then it changed the face of art for ever. As embroiderers we are fortunate, for not until we are quite sure that our perspective is correct, need we transfer our design to fabric (see Appendix B, Translating your sketches). While still at the design stage, we can experiment and move elements of the design until we are quite satisfied, as shown in Fig 10.

Etching, dashing and these simple rules of perspective are brought together in Plate 17, the study of a delightful thatched cottage in its well-tended garden.

PLATE 16 ▷

Detail of Plate 8. Bold etching and dashing form the impression of a solid, sturdy building while the planting in the foreground masks any eye-level features, such as traffic, which are not wanted in the finished picture. As in Plate 15, the large tree in the middle distance stands between the main subject and the shrubs in the foreground. Each sphere of planting is clearly defined

· · · · · · · · ·

Quite heavy etching has been employed on the thatch, in particular the window eaves, where the dashing stitches are bold and elongated. The walls of the cottage are almost obscured by planting, but where they are visible are conveyed by shorter fields of dashing. On this scale details of the garden's contents are necessarily impressionistic, but still those nearer to the house are higher in the perspective of the design, while the rockery, lilac and ornamental tree are lower on the canvas. A third element has been used to place the cottage solidly in its allotted space – from *behind* the building the branches of a tree appear to the left of the cottage, while above it a suggestion of sky is included.

PLATE 17 △

What may have begun life as a row of small cottages has by now often been converted into a single dwelling, with a well-tended garden taking the place of former vegetable plots and chicken runs. The art of thatching, once under threat, is now in the ascendant as many new country dwellers have come to appreciate the warm, insulative properties of Norfolk reed. Each master thatcher has his own personal motif which is incorporated in each of his roofs. Here, a simple inverted triangular pattern runs along the ridge, but often designs are far more elaborate
14 x 7.5cm (5½ x 3 inches)

◁ *Fig 10*
The lower the horizontal plane, the nearer it appears to bring the subject. The tree obscures part of the hedgerow which in turn recedes to the distance. The horizon is farthest away and therefore 'tops' the study

GUESTS AND LODGERS

The dwellings which make up a village are home not only to its human inhabitants. Year after year the swallows return, not just to the same village, but often to the eaves of the same cottage. Butterflies and other insects overwinter in undisturbed nooks and crannies, attics and cupboards, and animals make their homes where they may share in their hosts' unwitting hospitality.

Many people actively encourage the use of these 'shared facilities'. They fill their garden with butterfly-friendly shrubs, keep small areas of ground permanently damp so that in the driest spring the swallows can still find mud with which to build, and pride themselves on a bird table thoughtfully stocked with foodstuffs to tempt even the most garden-shy warbler. But free-loaders and gate-crashers will always spot a good party, and some of the most entertaining guests at any gathering may well be those without an invitation.

The starling is one of the most familiar birds in any garden; aggressive, raucous, gregarious and a shameful opportunist, it is also the comedian of the bird table, attempting a graceful glide-in landing and then overshooting its perch, announcing its arrival with a jumble of whistles and squeals. For years I have lived with successive generations of two starling families, one under the apex of each gable end of my cottage; their irrepressible nature has been an education. On close inspection they are not the dull, common-looking birds they appear. In summer, adults of both sexes have glossy plumage – black at a glance, but actually shot through with iridescent flashes of bottle-green, purple and royal blue (Plate 18). This is difficult to capture in embroidery, and the use of pure silk is an advantage, especially if a fine gauge is used, as a 3/1F or 4/1F thread can be made comprising two or three strands of black together with other strands in the appropriate colour. This then behaves identically to the feathers of the bird itself – and appears black under certain lighting conditions, while coming to life and showing its colour when caught in light from other directions.

A further dimension can be achieved by the use of blending filaments when making up the thread. Either a very fine metallic thread, or the coloured cellophane strip from a pre-formed specialist thread may be separated out and incorporated as a strand of 3/1F. Of course, it is important that a 'free' thread is used rather than a twist, as the shine created by the strata of radial stitching gives the study its liveliness.

The ticking (see Appendix A) on the head of the bird, and its pale, whitish markings become more evident in the winter when its plumage loses a little of its gaudiness, but even in the summer they are important features. These are created, in the former instance, by overlaying tiny ticking stitches on the head feathers, and for the larger markings, by working chevrons of Dalmatian-dog technique, to be surrounded by the main body of the work.

Indoor visitors are less common in these days of insulation, damp-proof courses and pest control. Yet, at certain times of the year migratory animals

PLATE 18 ▷

Sturnus vulgaris *is the Latin name for the starling – and vulgar he certainly is; but for all that the starling can be a valuable aid to the gardener and farmer as its diet is largely formed of wireworms, leather-jackets (the cocooned grub of the cranefly) and other agricultural pests. The black-and-yellow cranefly* (Nephrotoma maculosa)*, shown here on a sweet-pea flower, is slightly smaller than the more familiar daddy-long-legs, but equally damaging in the garden. Sweet peas* (Lathyrus odoratus) *are another favourite of the cottage garden, introduced into England in the late seventeenth century and hybridized into many brilliantly coloured and sweet-smelling varieties. They were immensely popular in Edwardian gardens, and were the special choice of Queen Alexandra for bouquets and posies. As with many members of the enormous pea family their growing habits make them a joy for the embroiderer as they twist and coil around themselves and whatever else may be near! When recreating the coiling habit of any climbing plant remember the 'before/behind' principle as the stems interweave: if the stem which originates nearest to you always appears in front of its counterpart you will not achieve the interlace. Follow the course of the topmost tendril in this study and you will see how it alternates as it works its way down the bamboo cane*

18 x 27cm (7 x 10½ inches)

HELEN
STEVENS

sometimes drop in by mistake (I live on an amphibians' through-way and occasionally find toads in the sitting room), but there is one animal whose unwilling association with man in the past is a legitimate excuse for its squatters' rights: the fat, or edible, dormouse was bred in captivity by the Romans who considered it be to a tasty and unusual meal; hence its name.

A native of southern Europe, and not a great traveller by inclination, it was transported throughout the Roman Empire (though not apparently into Britain) and escapees established colonies which thrived in the wild. In the early 1900s a few specimens were imported into the Home Counties of England as curiosities and released in Hertfordshire where in places they have become numerous enough to be regarded as a nuisance. They are basically woodland animals, but in the autumn enter houses and sheds to find winter quarters for hibernation and build up a store of food.

Like the starling, the fat dormouse is something of a comedian, and its antics in the attic, while creating enough scuttling, gnawing and squeaking to

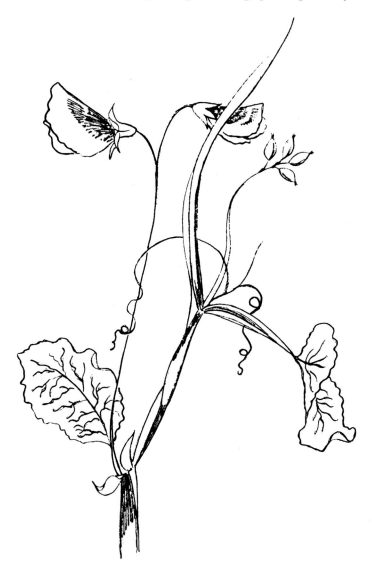

Fig 11 ▷
Sweet peas. Remember that to make a picture interesting there must be 'movement'. In a single 'still life' study this can still be achieved by allowing features to interlace and coil around themselves. Do not transfer fine details such as tendrils. These can be added to your embroidery freehand

HELEN STEVENS

◁ *PLATE 19*
Whiskers quivering, the edible dormouse (Glis glis) *is a charming, if occasionally noisy, uninvited guest. Larger than the common dormouse, it can be mistaken for a grey squirrel in its woodland habitat, but may be distinguished by the fact that its fat glossy tail is prehensile (grasping), and when sitting upright is laid flat along the ground – a squirrel's, of course, arches upward. All species of dormice are insectivorous as well as vegetarian, and butterflies (in this case small tortoiseshells) which start overwintering before the dormouse begins his hibernation may well never make it to the spring! The smooth, radial* opus plumarium *on the animal's body catches the light beautifully when worked in silk – an extension of this technique, river stitching, will be discussed in Chapter 2*
10.5 x 11.5cm (4 x 4½ inches)

keep residents in bedrooms below wide awake, can provide inspiration for the artist looking for an unusual subject. To complement a recent addition to the English countryside scene, why not try a modernist setting? The smooth, flowing stitches of the *opus plumarium* on the body make a very satisfying contrast with the straight rigid lines of the stylized struts and cables of the roof space, and a slightly surreal effect is created by the hibernating butterflies and cobweb.

Even in this unusual interpretation it is important not to lose sight of certain tricks which give a three-dimensional reality to the study. A light source, on this occasion at the top left-hand side of the picture, means that the animal needs a shadow line and the colouring of the struts should be graduated: lighter above and darker beneath. The struts and red cable are created by very long straight stitches, worked *after* the main body of the animal. A few fine silk stitches are then overlaid radiating at the same angle as the strata of *opus plumarium* to soften the edges of the animal's fur where it appears to cross the struts.

CHAPTER TWO

WAYFARERS ALL

It reminds me very much of Bilbo. He often used to say there was only one Road, that it was like a great river: its springs were at every doorstep, and every path was its tributary. You step into the Road and if you don't keep your feet there is no knowing where you might get swept off to.

The Fellowship of the Ring
J. R. R. Tolkien

HELEN
STEVENS

TO BE A PILGRIM

Long before there were human travellers there were tracks and runs through the countryside. Animals made regular forays from their living places to streams and rivers and to favourite hunting and eating grounds. Early man no doubt followed their example, but as he began to use stone and iron implements he was able to remove undergrowth and soil more easily and so the first purpose-built roads appeared.

The earliest identifiable roads kept to the high ground, and remnants of these prehistoric ridgeways can still be seen today. Often they are marked by monoliths, huge standing stones upon whose purpose we can only speculate. Tiny, sunken, winding lanes between tall hedgerows probably also date from an extremely early era and mark the boundaries of Celtic or Saxon settlements. Ditches were dug between settlements, the spoil heaped up on either side, and in later centuries, when the need for protection became less important, they began to be used as short cuts.

The Romans took little notice of boundaries! The straightness of their roads bears witness to the efficiency of the military mind. Their roads were mainly built on embankments to aid drainage, and the verges created either side of these highways formed an entirely new habitat for small animals and other wild creatures which is still an important element in today's countryside. There are thousands of acres of wayside verge in existence today – it seems odd that the busier the road, the less disturbed are the roadside residents by human interference – and many of our most common small mammals and wildflowers depend upon these areas.

Whether from ancient monolith to stone circle, or from cross to Christian shrine, an important aspect of the road has always been pilgrimage. Many of the great abbeys of the Middle Ages, so richly adorned with embroidery and tapestry, woven hangings and vestments, were ruined during the Reformation and we can only guess at the treasure trove of textiles which were destroyed with them, or 'liberated' during the process. Certain vestments, and fragments of embroidery reputed to have belonged to saints such as Thomas à Becket, St Edmund and St Cuthbert became, and still are, relics in their own right.

Ruins, and abbey ruins in particular, have a strange other-worldliness about them which translates effectively into embroidery. Perhaps it is the play of light and shadow, the variety of textures within the stone, the free rein which may be given to the imagination, which appeals – whatever the inspiration, the lessons learnt regarding etching, dotting and dashing should be applied here. For the first time, too, we can begin to explore the properties of climbing plants superimposed upon a subject in the middle distance. Compare the ivy spilling over the ruined wall in Plate 20 with the tree in the middle foreground on Plate 16 in the previous chapter. It is quite apparent in the former that the plant is actually *on* the wall, not free-standing or hanging.

◁ *PLATE 20*

Beside a country road the ruin of a once great abbey may now consist only of a few overgrown stone arches and columns. Where weary pilgrims found shelter only the birds make their homes (yellow wagtails, Motacilla flava) *and the once dusty lane is now metalled, its ancient course still winding between high hedgerows. Deep shadows under the stone arches are created by bold areas of black dashing, lightening in two abrupt strata as sunlight reaches the old, flaking stonework. Similar dashing, though this time horizontal, describes the surface of the road, interrupted by surface puddles and ruts. The meandering course of the road is echoed by a suggestion of the sky leading the eye off into infinity*

Embroidery shown life size:
22.5 x 21cm (8¾ x 8¼ inches)

PLATE 21 △

*Detail of Plate 20. By overlaying the
embroidered ivy (or other climbing plants)
directly on to the already existing dot, dash or
etching stitch, the effect is created of one feature
actually being in contact with the next*

This is achieved in two ways, the first at design stage. When a feature is free-standing, such as a tree in front of a wall, prepare the sketch (or tracing) of the tree first and then sketch in the wall as a backdrop behind it (see Fig 12). You will find that a small halo naturally forms around the foremost feature, as you avoid, naturally, sketching into an existing motif. When creating ivy climbing a wall, sketch the wall first in its entirety and then scribble in the rough position of the ivy, over the top of your existing pencil work. You may find it easier if you have two pencils, a multipurpose HB for the body of the work, and a much softer lead, such as 2B or 3B to rough in the superimposed feature (see Fig 13). When these elements are transferred on to your fabric you will find that the halo is also transferred, and the ivy appears as a darker mass than its surroundings (if necessary press a little harder to transfer this feature, see Appendix A).

Both these tips serve as reminders when the actual embroidery is underway, for it is important to keep your original sketch by you. Work the wall first, whether in dotting or dashing. Do not work beyond the halo around the tree, but work right over the indication of the ivy. We will discuss the detailed working of trees later. Turning to the climbing plant, it is now possible, by referring to your sketch for an indication of where it should appear, to work first the twisting stems of the ivy, and then the individual leaves in a tiny seed stitch right over the existing work (see Plate 21). There will be absolutely none of the background fabric visible. When the tree is worked, however, it will be embroidered straight on to the background fabric and a certain amount of this will show through the embroidery. This 'air' or nothingness will convey a feeling of space between the tree and the wall, so that it appears to be standing in front of that feature, separated by some distance. This rule applies even in the far distance (see Plate 22). The tree at the end of the green is a considerable distance from the viewer, the building beyond even further – but it still appears to be free-standing, there is no confusion even in long-shot.

Fig 12 △
It may look strange in sketch form, but leave a 'halo' around a foreground feature to define it as being in front of the background elements. Transfer it similarly

Fig 13 △
To indicate that a plant is climbing on a wall, sketch the background first, and then superimpose the new feature. It is useful to have pencils of varying softness – from 2H to 2B – to create differing effects

△ *PLATE 22*
Detail of Plate 8. In contrast to Plate 21, working the two features entirely separately, as shown here, and leaving a small amount of background fabric visible, gives an impression of intervening space

SAINTS AND SINNERS

Chaucer's Canterbury pilgrims were typical of many early road-users. They travelled in groups for safety, broke their journeys frequently and were an ill-assorted party from all walks of life. Roads were dangerous places, it was better to start the day's journey at dawn and begin to look for the next night's lodging by midday. Some wayside plants still have country names which bear witness to this practice (Plate 23). 'Jack-go-to-bed-at-noon' was a name given to goat's beard, also known as the pilgrim or Joseph's flower, the former because its bright flowers opened at daybreak and closed in the early afternoon, the second because the silky tufts which appear after the flower has died were said to look like a beard – and the Virgin's husband was invariably shown as bearded.

The flower of the goat's beard is unexceptional, a round dandelion-type head with long sepals, but the leaves and fruiting body are a joy for embroiderers. Each long, grass-like leaf sheaths the stem individually, the larger leaves towards the base of the plant often reflexing and coiling delightfully, forming an immensely decorative motif. Study the anatomy of the leaves carefully; in order to recreate the flexes and twists, opposite angle stitching must be used and where the stem appears to sink down into the sheath, shading will give the effect of depth (see Fig 14).

The goat's beard's clock differs from that of the dandelion in several ways. First, it is larger and yet comprised of far fewer individual parachutes. The downy filaments of the parachutes are slightly irregular (on the dandelion they are much more regimented). Seen to best advantage on black, the clock can be worked using the finest thread available. Draw the head by outlining a circle and filling it with as many rosettes of filaments as necessary to build up the whole. When transferring the design on to fabric do not impress the whole of the motif, only the dot at the centre of each parachute (the technique is identical for a common dandelion clock, see *The Embroiderer's Countryside*) and then embroider each rosette or parachute as a series of straight radial stitches, first in the fine gauge, then, to build up the body slightly, incorporating a few strands of creamy, slightly thicker thread. Finally a touch of gold at the centre of each (seed stitching) and the clock is complete. Contrasted by the compact, bullet-shaped heads of plantian the ethereal quality of the goat's beard is emphasized; it may be complemented by the equally delicate wings of the muslin moth *(Diaphora mendica)*, which as its name suggests has almost transparently fragile, white wings.

It is unusual to be able to work an entire butterfly or moth in a single colour, but here it can be done. Using once again the finest thread available (silk, if possible) the entire wing can be worked in a single stratum of radial stitches, sloping steeply towards the moth's body. Then, using a white blending filament incorporating a colourless cellophane strip, work a very narrow border of straight stitches around the outside of each wing. Lastly, separate out the cellophane strand from a further length of blending filament and overlay it at random on the

PLATE 24 ▷
*Charlatans and rogues – believing that
unwary travellers might be more easily parted
from their money by genuine 'Egyptians'
(Gypsies) – daubed their bodies with the sap of
the gipsywort* (Lycopus europaeus) *which
effectively dyed their skin a swarthy brown.
Others, to arouse sympathy, rubbed their limbs
with the irritant sap produced by the
traveller's joy* (Clematis vitalba) *which
produced the appearance of weeping – though
apparently painless – ulcers. The spectacular
lilac-pink whorls of florets on the gipsywort can
be spangled with seed stitches in a darker pink
to indicate stamens which thrust out of each
cluster as it forms at the base of a pair of
leaves. 'Faeries' crowns' and 'gypsies'
garlands' are country names for these whorls*
12 x 26cm (4¾ x 10¼ inches)

main field of the wing, following exactly the direction of the original stitches. Do not draw the stitches of the silk or the filament too tightly; allow them to lie on the background fabric with no tension, and they will naturally separate slightly in places allowing the black fabric to show through, thus enhancing the diaphanous effect of muslin suggested by the moth's name.

The idea of allowing thread to lie loosely on the background fabric, and, by falling into natural waves and curves, create new effects is one that can be explored further in Plate 24. The coiling traveller's joy is a plant which can be included in a variety of designs to add interest and movement to a study. Here it is shown with gipsywort, another flower common along country roadsides, particularly close to rivers. The two plants make an attractive combination: one fluid and soft, the other vigorous and erect. The seeds of the traveller's joy are clustered at the end of flower stalks and each is surmounted by a long feathery plume, which, caught by the wind, eventually bears it away like a kite with a long fluttering tail.

To create these fluffy cotton-wool balls it is necessary to allow the thread to lie freely on the fabric, while still anchored in place. Work the seeds at the core of the ball first (see Fig 15 (top)). With a fine thread, preferably floss silk, take a long stitch from one of the seeds to a point about 2.5cm (1 inch) away from the head. Put a finger under the thread to keep it away from the background fabric and take a very small stitch at the outer point to bring the thread back to the surface of the fabric (Fig 15 (centre)). Take a third stitch back to the seed head, again keeping a finger beneath the thread to keep it loose. Remove your finger and two long loops will run from the seed head to the outer point. Repeat the process clockwise around the head until a corona of long, loose stitches is in place (Fig 15 (bottom)) and check that none of the thread is hanging loose on the back of the work. In a study such as Plate 24 it is best if this process is left until the rest of the work is complete, as the 'floating stitches' are fragile and may easily be snagged. Great care must also be taken during mounting and framing (see Appendix B).

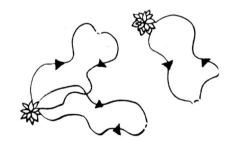

The same technique may also be used to good effect on a pale background fabric, and here it becomes obvious why such a small stitch must be taken at the outer limit of the corona. On a fine pale ground, threads on the reverse of the work can be seen through the material, which would clearly spoil the effect. For

Fig 15 ▷
Top: Work the core of the seed head first
Centre: Take long, loose stitches outward, a
tiny stitch on the reverse, and another long
stitch back to the head. Arrows show the
direction of each stitch
Bottom: Work your way around the head,
allowing the loops to fall where they please —
overlapping one another or recoiling, they will
imitate the actual plant

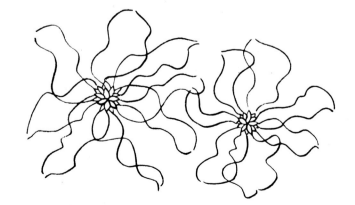

PLATE 25 ▷

*The tenacious clematis will climb up any sturdy
host and the rigid stems of the teasel
(Dispascus fullonum) are ideal. From the
Old English taesel meaning 'to card, tear or
tease', it is clear from its name that the plant's
use in the textile trade goes back many
centuries, certainly to the era of* Opus
Anglicanum. *The folk names of 'barber's
brushes', 'prickly beehives' and 'brushes and
combs' are even more readily understandable.
When in flower, like the plantain, the tiny
florets form in a circlet around the head and
move downwards as those above die off (see
Fig 16). Seeds form in the bristly sepals, which
are a favourite food for many birds, especially
goldfinches (*Carduelis carduelis*). The clearly
defined markings on the upper body of the
goldfinch are an ideal subject for sharply
delineated strata of radial stitching, while the
underparts are the exact opposite, golden-buff
colouring merging smoothly into cream. A
study such as this emphasizes the importance of
widening your palette of colours – apart from
the startling red, yellow and black, almost the
whole picture is worked in shades of gold,
cream and ecru*
12 x 32cm (4¾ x 12½ inches)

the same reason, in all your work on a pale background, be sure to weave the loose 'tails' back into the body of the embroidery when finishing off.

Plate 25 is another picture concentrating upon contrast for its theme; the soft, downy balls of clematis alternating with the spiky, prickly heads of the teasels. The wild teasel *(Dispascus fullonum)* is very similar to the fuller's teasel, cultivated for centuries for use in the textile industry, the spines on the end of the bracts curving backwards only slightly less vigorously. It is a complicated plant shape, but one which can be captured in embroidery if taken apart and reconstructed piece by piece. The teasel head is shown in detail in Plate 26, and sketched in Fig 16.

To create your design, first rough out an oval shape, and then sketch in a series of spines (remembering that those facing you will reflex), together with the long, curving bracts at the base of the head. When the design is transferred on to your fabric, work the oval head first, using chevron stitch (see Appendix A) to create the prickles and infilling the head where necessary with perpendicular straight stitches. Work the bracts in snake stitch (Appendix A) before the final wicked spines are superimposed on to the chevron stitches which will, in places, lie over other features. Short, stubby prickles cover the brittle stems of the plant. These are not pronounced enough to require chevron stitching, but a short, angular stitch, duly shadow-lined at strategic places along the stem, will create the effect of a rough, scratchy surface.

WORKERS, MIGRANTS AND IMMIGRANTS

Footsore and travel-weary, the medieval pilgrim had to make the most of whatever could be found along the way to make his trip more bearable, and today we can still benefit from his example. Milfoil, or yarrow (Plate 27), is a plant to 'foil a thousand plots' – the common man's explanation for the Latin name *millefolium*, but none the less apposite for that. The Anglo-Saxons used the plant to staunch and heal wounds, drive away sickness and increase sexual attraction while protecting from romantic mishaps. On a more practical level it was a remedy for running sores and was picked by travellers to ease the pain of blisters.

The flowers are usually creamy, but often flushed with pink. At the core of each tiny floret is a minute pincushion of pollen which appears to be spangled with gold dust. This type of flower works well on a black background, as discussed at Plate 12b (page 21), but it is also a delightfully delicate subject worked on a pale ground. In a very detailed study such as this, it is particularly important that the shadow line should be worked effectively, as without it the outline of the flowers and stems would lack all definition. A single strand of very fine black silk is all that is needed to create this effect, and remember that where the stems of the florets branch away from each other, the shadow line should always remain on the lower edge of the fork.

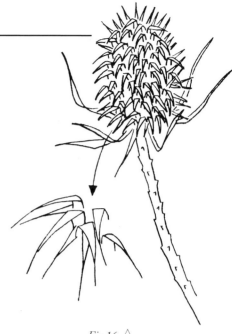

Fig 16 △
The head of the teasel is a mass of chevron stitching – (see Appendix A)

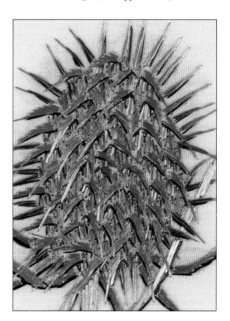

PLATE 26 △
Detail of Plate 25. In close up the teasel-head appears to be some fantastic alien life form! By reflexing the spines on the body of the teasel (as we see it) to the right and the left, and those apparently projecting from the edges straight out, an impression of the roundness of the subject is created. Water trapped inside the cups of the teasel was thought to have curative properties and was often used as an eye-wash

. . . .

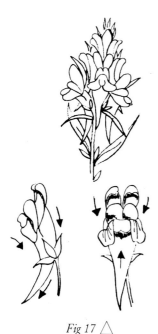

Fig 17 △

The complex shapes which make up the flower of the toadflax. The head comprises numerous florets so analyse a single bloom before attempting to put together the whole. Arrows indicate directional stitching – and do not forget the shadow line and other shaded areas

PLATE 27 ▷

Unlike the solitary mason bees (Plate 13), bumble bees (here the white tailed Bombus lucorum*) live in colonies but whereas the domestic honey beehive may contain up to 50,000 bees, bumbles rarely exceed 150. Their colonies do not make enough honey to survive the winter. The workers, drones and old queen all die in the autumn, and young fertilized queens disperse to hibernate and found new colonies in the spring. Late-flowering perennials such as the milfoil are important sources of energy. The name* millefolium *actually refers to the plant's 'thousand' feathery leaves, strongly divided into many narrow segments. These must be worked very freely in straight stitching, which radiates initially from the side veins and then the central vein of the main leaf core. (It can be tricky to maintain this directional flow, but similarly difficult leaf subjects will be discussed in the next chapter)*
8.5 x 9.5cm (3¼ x 3¾ inches)

The nectar and pollen of the milfoil is attractive to bees – in an intimate study such as this details of continuity are important. Remember to work the bees' pollen sacs in the same shade as the core of the flowers!

Nicholas Culpeper's famous herbal, written in the seventeenth century, reports that a poultice made from milfoil and toadflax proved to be of great relief to those suffering discomfort of the rear – clearly travellers on horseback as well as on foot were often in need of assistance – and both common and pale toadflax can still be seen along old tracks and bridleways (Plate 28).

The flowers of the toadflax are complex and need to be analysed before embroidery can begin, as in Fig 17. As with most flowers, the simplest rule applies: begin at the centre and work your way outwards. The throat of the flower extends behind the sepals into a spur. This must be regarded as the growing point, towards which all the radial stitching must flow. Work the yellow-orange lips first, then the heart-shaped upper and lower 'petals', and finally the spur. By contrast, the buds, leaves and fruiting bodies are all simple shapes.

Culpeper's opinion of toadflax's virtues were formed long after its name had become widely adopted – it was once regarded as being so useless as to be fit only for toads, the same word, in common with 'dog', was applied to other apparently worthless plants. The common toad, however, was regarded as the traveller's friend and it was good luck to have one cross your path. Easter pilgrims must occasionally have been overwhelmed by good fortune, as the migration of the toad

HELEN
STEVENS

◁ *PLATE 28*
While the common and pale toadflax
(Linaria) *are tall thrusting plants, the more*
delicate ivy-leaved toadflax (Cymbalaria
muralis) *has long, trailing stems which need*
support. It was introduced from the
Mediterranean into London in 1640, as a
garden plant but quickly spread and in 350
years has colonized Great Britain. The
derivation of its common name is self evident.
The ivy-shaped leaves may be worked in a
single stratum of opus plumarium *radiating*
sharply inwards towards a short central vein
and describing almost a complete 360 degree
turn. Travellers in the featureless
Cambridgeshire fens once believed that if a
dagger was placed lightly on the skin of the
common toad (Bufo bufo), *it would turn to*
face north. Try to keep a sense of direction and
light in an unusual study such as this,
emphasizing the solidity of the toad (in contrast
to the fragility of the plants) by blocking in an
area of shadow under the animal.
The horizontal ground stitches are contrasted
by the simple straight stitches of the
grasses to the left, which lead the eye upwards
to the rest of the study
12 x 19cm (4¾ x 7½ inches)

. . . .

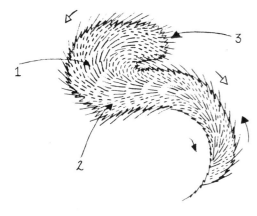

Fig 18 △

River stitch. In all cases the black arrows indicate the sweep of the stitching, while the open arrows show the direction in which individual stitches must be taken. The central core of the tail is worked first (1), followed by the outer strata (2). Finally, the whole motif is softened by overlaying fine straight stitches (3)

PLATE 29 ▷

Few things are prettier than the wild daffodil (Narcissus pseudonarcissus) *and the familiar snowdrop* (Galanthus nivalis), *but mastering their complex forms requires careful analysis of direction and shadow*
16 x 20.5cm (6¼ x 8 inches)

population in March or April was, and still is, often a spectacular affair. Hundreds of toads leave their winter quarters after hibernation to make their way to breeding grounds, allowing no obstacle to stand in their way. Today, many are killed by cars, and the clean fairly deep water which they need to spawn is becoming less common as ponds are drained for agriculture or polluted by farm chemicals.

Toads are welcomed by knowledgeable gardeners, as they eat many insect pests. If you are fortunate enough to find one (they often spend daylight hours sheltering under dense bedding plants) touch it gently with your fingertips to explore the unique texture of its skin: dry, warm and pimply. Often described as 'warty', the term hardly does justice to this beautiful animal, which can vary in colour from warm loamy brown to olive green. Oddly, some of the techniques which we have learnt for use on buildings can be applied here to create a matt, grainy effect. The toad's body is more richly textured on its upper parts than lower, but because it is uniformly marked and textured on all the upper surfaces, the legs, for instance, would appear to merge into the rest of the body unless outlined. Ignoring, for once, the principle of only outlining the shadow line, work a wavy line of short stitches to outline the legs, back foot (or feet) and eye sockets. With careful attention to the variation in colour of the markings, use dotting or seeding stitches to work your way down the body – large stitches towards the top, decreasing in size until they reach the relative smoothness of the belly. The beautiful golden eye can be highlighted to focus upon some other feature of the picture – such as an unwary fly!

The grey squirrel, often seen along tree-lined country roads, suburban avenues and even in city parks, is a true immigrant. A native of the eastern United States, it was introduced into Britain in the mid-nineteenth century and has rapidly become one of the most familiar, non-hibernating small mammals. In common with many animals which remain active during the winter its coat changes colour and texture as the seasons turn: from a grey-brown, grizzled gold in the summer to bright silver flecked with gunmetal-grey flanks and caramel-coloured head, feet and hackles in the winter, as shown in Plate 29.

Radial *opus plumarium* is, as has been discussed, a perfect technique to convey the smooth sweep of an animal's body fur from nose to haunch. It can sweep around the hind leg to complete a 360 degree turn, merging effortlessly with the body of the stitches above. Beginning at the nose of the animal the strata of stitches sweep out smoothly like the ripples around a pebble thrown into water. However, this technique does not work so satisfactorily when the field to be covered does not curve continuously in the same direction. The squirrel's tail is a good example. From the animal's rump, it sweeps first to the left and then sharply right, but at all times must continue to appear fluffy, though with a solid underlying structure.

Work the main body of the animal first, from the head downwards as usual. The 'core' of the tail may then be embroidered, as a narrow band of *opus plumarium* running up the centre of the field to be filled, from the rump, towards

the tip. On either side of this core, work wedges of the usual fan-shaped sections of radial stitching (if you have a wide choice of shades, use the lighter ones on the unshadowed side of the tail, and vice versa). Where the tail curves over and changes direction, on the inside of the curve decrease the angle of the wedge, and on the outside of the curve increase it. The flow of stitches will continue apparently unbroken: continuing the watery analogy, we will call this 'river stitch'. Finally, to emphasize the fluffiness of the subject, overlay the whole feature with single strands of silk projecting beyond the edges of the existing stitching, and superimposed over any background elements of the design. A few similar strokes in fine black thread on the shadowed edges of the tail and it is complete. This order of working is noted in Fig 18.

The grey squirrel's diet is very varied. Together with nuts, fungi, beech-mast, acorns and whatever he may be offered by humans, leaves, green shoots, bark, bulbs, flowers and buds are all on the menu. In February the wild daffodil and snowdrop come into bloom and the first taste of spring may be savoured. These two flowers have, of course, become garden favourites, though increasingly rare in the wild, and make easy subjects for study if picked from the garden (the uncultivated varieties are protected by law).

Neither the daffodil nor the snowdrop are easy flowers to interpret. Both have outer whorls of sepals protecting inner petals or coronas which means that deep shadows form where the two overlap. On the snowdrops this can be conveyed simply by using grey thread in place of white on the undersides of the protective 'skirts', the pretty petticoats beneath highlighted by their pale-green markings. The daffodil, on the other hand, needs closer attention if it is not to appear flat and uninteresting. The long trumpet-shaped corona curves outwards at its lip and, the shadow line having been carefully worked out, it is important to get the directional stitching right (see Fig 19). The deep throat of the trumpet needs to be shadowed in dark grey – the first stratum of radial stitching – followed immediately by a second stratum of yellow. This creates a too stark cut-off line between the two strata which must be softened by shooting stitches (see Appendix A) of grey worked smoothly into the yellow. The outer surface of the trumpet may then be worked, the stitches radiating from the base of the sepals. Each sepal may then be worked similarly in grey and yellow. The papery spathe which protects the bud before it opens remains covering the lower neck of the flower. It is important that this is not overlooked at design stage, as it is one of the features which give the daffodil its unmistakable character. Seen to better advantage on the bud, it can be worked simply in straight *opus plumarium*.

Two hundred years ago the scene depicted in Plate 29 could not have existed. The grey squirrel and the native plants of Britain were separated by the Atlantic Ocean. For better or for worse mankind's exploration of the world has generated strange bedfellows. For the embroiderer, seeking out unusual combinations of subject matter and evolving techniques to capture their qualities is an unending voyage of discovery.

Fig 19 △
Arrows indicate the direction of stitching.
Shadowing is important both on the wild
daffodil and the more delicate narcissus

CHAPTER THREE

BARNS, BARLEY AND BEER

*The grass was June high and had come up
with a rush, a massed entanglement of species,
crested with flowers and spears of wild wheat
Mr Jones's pond was bubbling with life
The lane itself was crusted with cow dung, hard
baked and smelling good.*

Cider with Rosie
Laurie Lee

HELEN
STEVENS

SUNSHINE AND SHADOWS

Just before twilight on hot summer evenings, the barn owl will make a preliminary circuit of his favourite hunting ground. Golden brown suede above, soft white velvet below, he swoops silently from barn or hollow tree, wings outstretched, black eyes searching the long grass for the tell-tale movement of mouse or vole. The barn owl was once a common bird of the British countryside, living in harmony with man – many farmers had special 'owl windows' built under the eaves of their barns, as the owls were valuable allies in the war against vermin. Modern farming methods have meant the loss of many traditional barns, and numbers have declined. Where old barns and grassy headlands survive barn owls still find a home (Plate 32).

For the country embroiderer a scene such as this has a powerful appeal. The barn, the pond, the dominant central tree offer a variety of textures and techniques which build into a delightful whole. The long grass by the barn door, the jumble of wildflowers in the mid-foreground, the final rounding off of the design by the dog roses are each treated differently, and each adds to the overall success of the picture.

We have already discussed on page 37 how to create the effect of a plant clinging to a building (here it is used where the creeper climbs up the side of the barn) and how to place another feature some distance away towards the foreground of the picture (page 37), but how, in a distant perspective, can we work fine details such as long grasses effectively and include realistic splashes of colour? The answer lies again in the use of contrast and a strict order of working. In front of the barn, along the hedgerow and around the pond, long grass softens the edges of all three features. The best rule to follow is, as ever, the simplest – work the background features first and then superimpose the grasses in fine thread, beginning with those which are distant and working forwards. This is seen most clearly in front of the barn (Plate 31).

Using as fine a gauge as possible, and in a slightly deeper shade closer to the building, work short upright straight stitches in a line across the base of the wall. (Although they are worked in the same *direction* as the dashing of the wall, a change in *texture*, from 2/1T to single floss will provide the contrast.) Work a second line of slightly longer stitches in front of these, then a third and so on. The nature of the stitching will allow a small amount of the background fabric to show through the embroidery, and the effect of space and movement will be created.

Working the grasses along the hedgerow is easier – simply superimpose the straight stitching fairly randomly along the base of the other shrubs – but around the pond more care must be taken as to the order of working. Embroider the water first. For a small area such as this, a fine floss will create an effect of shine and reflection. On the near bank, where the grasses appear to lie across the water, superimpose them, but on the far bank, where the grasses appear to lie over the features beyond, work *those* elements next. Then work the straight stitching

◁ *PLATE 30*

The barn owl (Tyto alba) *occurs in both a dark and lighted chested form, both equally dramatic. The broad, barred wings create a bold sweep of movement; worked in smooth floss silk they catch every nuance of light giving the impression of an almost infinite variety of grey shading. An unusual, surreal addition to the picture is the inclusion of the owl window, a cruciform hole in a highly textured and stylized section of wall. Dotting and dashing in both silk and wool is interspersed with surface couched fibres. Experiment with your designs – don't be afraid to include the unexpected, both in perspective and content*

Embroidery shown life size:
16 x 21.5cm (6¼ x 8½ inches)

directly from the bank of the pond up, over the more distant motifs (see Fig 20). Splashes of colour can be included in the shape of bright red, yellow or pink seed stitches in among the grasses. Like the quick dab of an impressionist's paintbrush, they will appear to be distant poppies, corn marigolds and mallow.

The towering lime tree is typical of many planted close to barns, not only to give shade, but also for protection – in earlier centuries, country folk believed that the lime was a holy tree with the power to overcome the evil eye. Near to a grain store it would prevent the grain from going mouldy, or livestock from being cursed. In Plate 32, the main trunk has been attacked by ivy, and in places the upper branches are already beginning to show the tell-tale signs of strangulation – and in doing so partly reveal the structure of the tree.

In embroidery, a tree must 'grow' just as it does in nature, the trunk, branches and twigs worked first and then clothed by leaves worked, in this case, in slightly elongated seed stitching. Straight stitching (in fact, a delicate form of dashing) is used on the main trunk; branches are worked similarly and then

PLATE 32 ▷
'The Old Barn'. While the main focus of attention in this picture is the barn and its pond, the study is thrown into relief, and 'framed' by a variety of wildflowers, worked in some detail, although at a distance. For the sake of reality, it is important to be able to identify these flowers, although they have been miniaturized, and to do this it is necessary to emphasize their individuality both at design stage and in the completed embroidery. In the clump to the right, common mallow, rosebay willowherb, meadow cranesbill, cow parsley, curled dock and great mullein are all readily recognizable. In Fig 20 they are sketched as they would appear from a distance of about 120ft (36m). Obviously fine details such as stamens and bracts cannot be seen, but in the final embroidery they should be suggested by the appropriate touches of colour – yellow flecks on the willowherb, dark purple streaks on the mallow and russet-red splashes as the leaves of the cranesbill begin to turn. Echo the colours of these foreground plants with impressionistic dabs in the distant long grass, drawing the eye into the picture and retaining a sense of continuity
34.5 x 28cm (13½ x 11 inches)

◁*PLATE 31*
Detail of Plate 32. Long grasses recede towards the open barn doors. At this distance it is impossible to identify flowers other than by their colour and general habit. To the right of the doors wild honeysuckle clambers up the wall, its flowers clotted-cream yellow amid true green foliage. To the left the huge white trumpets of the large bindweed appear as elongated seed stitches in dark and light yellow-green leaves. Sunlight catches the edge of an indistinguishable object inside the barn, adding a little mystery to the scene

HELEN
STEVENS

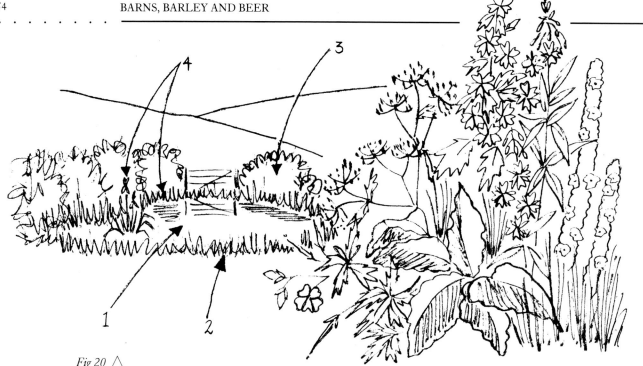

Fig 20 △

*Certain elements of Plate 32 have been used
here to illustrate the order of working. Work
foreground features such as the clump of wildflowers first and then the landscape elements in
sequence, ie, water, grasses to the front of the
pond, hedges, etc, to the rear and finally grasses
and plants between the water and the hedge*

Fig 21 △

*Radial stitching treating each eye as a core sets
the owl apart as a subject. The two opposing
strata of stitches meet in a ridge between the
eyes, sweep down over the bridge of the beak
and finally open out into a single radial
stratum to form the rest of the heart-shaped
face. Use the sketched lines as a guide for
directional stitching*

individual twigs separate the leaf growth. The characteristics of various species will be discussed later, but here the long slender branches arch upwards, very slightly inclining to the right, following the curve of the foreground rose and leading the eye towards the flying owl, which in turn swoops towards the centre of the picture, completing the overall 'movement' of the design. It is important that the elements of a large picture such as this are not disjointed, but flow smoothly, one to another.

Plate 32 is a study in sunlight – the barn owl on his first foray – but to appreciate this beautiful bird in his full glory, 'Old Hushwing' , as some country people call him, must be seen at night. Against black the barn owl is a perfect subject to explore the technique of 'softened feather work': ghostly white, his only underside markings are tear-drops and subdued bars of grey. Somehow we must capture that whispering, downy flight by enlarging upon the familiar rules of *opus plumarium*.

Working on black, of course, we need not outline, but voiding and subdued voiding (see Appendix A) is necessary to separate wing feathers and parts of the body – and subdued voiding gives the key to the softening of the feather work. Where the markings are large enough, work them in Dalmatian-dog technique, on smaller areas use ticking. Embroider the main body of the bird in radial *opus plumarium* and then, with the same fine thread used to 'subdue' the voiding, overlay the entire body of the work with straight directional stitching, similar to that used on the tail of the grey squirrel in Plate 29. This is particularly effective on the heart-shaped face of the bird (see Fig 21), shown in Plate 30, creating the ridge along the centre of the face and softening what would otherwise be a sharp, unnatural contour.

Fig 22 △
Little owls enjoy a tasty moth. Place the
highlight (formed by a tiny white seed stitch
worked over the black pupil) in the same
position relative to each eye so that a 'bead'
may be drawn to the object on which attention
is focused

◁ PLATE 33
The little owl has enjoyed something of a success
story since its introduction to Britain from the
mainland Europe in the nineteenth century.
Tolerant of man, it not only nests in farmland,
but also parks, quarries and orchards – in fact
anywhere a cosy hollow may be found. Its
small size, only 22cm (8½ inches long) makes
it an ideal subject for a small embroidered
study – but make sure all the component parts
of your design are to scale. The flowers shown
here are bindweed Convolvulus arvensis,
each flower of which is less than 2.5cm (1 inch
across), rather than the larger hedge bindweed
which would swamp the picture. The dead
branch is worked in straight opus
plumarium, *lighter above and darker as it*
approaches its shadow line
8.5 x 11cm (3¼ x 4¼ inches)

Plate 33 shows a little owl *(Athene noctua)*, another bird which, given the opportunity, will nest in barns and other farm buildings. Its markings are, for the embroiderer, a mass of Dalmatian spots, ticking and softening to create the impression of a fluffy little bird – with a permanently cross expression! As with the study of the barn owl, the wide-open eyes of the bird are partly obscured by its feathers (creating, in this case, the frown). When highlighting the eye, by adding a small white stitch, strategically placed, make sure that it is positioned at a similar angle relative to each eye. If this is not achieved the stare will appear glassy, or cross-eyed. You can experiment with the highlight at design stage by drawing a bead from each eye to an imaginary spot (see Fig 22).

HEATWAVE

Some farmland, if it is not too tightly straightjacketed by modern regimes, retains and in places conserves as useful many ancient features of the landscape which might otherwise have been drained, levelled or eroded away to nothing. Water meadows produce the most lush grass for grazing cattle; knolls, tuns and old spinneys of hawthorn offer protection to sheep on the high moors and echoes of the Ice Age remain as watering holes and ponds. The 'pingos' of the East Anglian Brecks were formed as glaciers receded, filled with water, survived through the aeons of dense forest finally cleared by the Saxons and today in the flat, sandy Breckland provide havens of shelter and food for many species of bird, insect and animal – and a rich variety of plant life from the humble daisy to the exotic white water-lily (Plate 34).

Unlike most species of grebe, the black-necked grebe requires its breeding place to be fringed with a rich growth of plants, both waterside and semi-submerged, which attract the insects and larvae upon which it prefers to feed. This glorious entanglement of flowers, grasses and reeds, the spectacular water plants and insects, and the grebes themselves make an irresistible combination of colour and design. You can almost sense the hazy, hot afternoon humming with the whir of iridescent wings and the gentle lap of the water as the bird drifts lazily from one clump of weed to the next. How is it possible to capture such an atmosphere?

There are three elements in a picture such as this – air, land and water. In the air, all is activity, the insects dance and the tall heads of the common clubrush sway. Lower down are 'land' elements, the shorter grasses and wildflowers intermingle and entwine, each busily doing its best to reach sun and air before the next. On the water, all is languid; the bird is elegant, the chick hides behind its parent, the water-lily floats serenely as a little water laps gently into its great saucer-shaped leaf. Each element must be treated differently.

The frenetic activity of the air is embroidered in the finest gauge of thread; it is light, ethereal, almost transparent. The dragonfly is shown, not symmetrically spread, but at an angle of flight, its legs reaching out towards the hapless mayfly. Use the honeycomb technique (see Appendix A) to work the wings (the order of working angled wings is the same as that for the butterfly in Fig 5 on page 19), but do not attempt to work honeycomb over honeycomb. Allow one wing to be complete with the others disappearing behind it. The mayflies' wings are worked similarly to bees' wings – their bodies, in common with the dragonfly's segmented into head, thorax and abdomen.

Until Victorian times, when the famous painting 'Moses in the Bulrushes' served to perpetuate the error that the reedmace was, in fact, a bulrush (see Fig 23), the common clubrush *(Schoenoplectus lacustris)* was known by that name – so called in medieval herbals for the good reason that it is so much bigger than other rushes. Its chestnut-brown flower spike is a mass of dense, bobbing heads borne

PLATE 34 ▷

'The Pingo'. In its breeding plumage, the black-necked grebe (Podiceps nigricollis) *is a spectacular bird. Although rare, it can occasionally be seen on man-made stretches of water, where it may breed for a single season before moving on to more remote locations. The chicks, with their dark and light grey striped down, rarely stray far from parent birds, their most distinctive feature an orange-red eye-patch. Peeping from behind the adult bird the chick here must appear camouflaged and yet distinct. As in nature, the striped markings echo the grassy bank of the pond, its fuzzy outline softened by allowing the fine straight stitches of its plumage to overlie the grasses behind it, while stitches forming the mother's downy, russet-red underparts are subtly superimposed. The white water lily* (Nymphaea alba) *has a variety of beautiful country names ('swan among the flowers' and 'lady of the lake' are typical), but to the Elizabethans it was 'nenuphar', a word derived from the ancient Sanskrit language. Look for water lilies to sketch on still water throughout Britain – but time your arrival carefully! The blooms open only at around noon, and close, partly disappearing below the water, before evening approaches*

32 x 31cm (12½ x 12¼ inches)

on a slender, sinuous stem. This plant serves to link the 'air' with the grasses and wildflowers below – an impression reinforced by the dancing gnats at its foot. The long, straight-stitched grasses, mainly in a 2/1T cotton, begin here and continue behind the body of the bird, leading on to the flowers at the right of the picture. Sedges differ from the grasses in that they have solid, often three-sided stems, and the flowering bodies are denser with more easily differentiated seeds. They are a pleasing motif in embroidery, and can be worked quite quickly in a number of ways. Small, oval-shaped seeds may be worked alternately on either side of the stem for a large-seeded sedge or a type of traditional fishbone stitch might be used for a finer sedge (Fig 24). These stitches can then be peppered over with tiny dot stitches of yellow or brown for the stamens and pollen. Water forget-me-nots, poppies and daisies complete the sweep.

Here, there is a greater expanse of water – at closer range – than in the distant pool in Plate 32, and it is worked in 2/1T silk. The water is still, and best conveyed as simply as possible through straight, horizontal blocking. There is a ripple of water shown through the strata of differing colours used.

Working the grebe is straightforward – the use of radial *opus plumarium* creates the smooth upper and lower body, and the only remarkable features are the spectacular golden ear-tufts and the softened feathering from the fluffy underparts extending slightly over the smooth brown upper body. The head and

◁ *Fig 24*

Sedges. The common cottongrass, flowering in detail (top), shown in the middle distance as its fruiting body ripens into 'cotton' (bottom left), and common sedge (bottom centre and right)

Fig 23 △

The head of the clubrush (top) works well as a 'close up' motif, sinuous and finely drawn, but the bulrush (bottom) with its stocky head and thick, upright stems is better used as a subject in the middle distance where the whole of the plant can be included

PLATE 35 △

*Water lilies have been so hybridized over the
last two centuries for ornamental water
features in parks and gardens that a huge
variety of colours and forms are available.*
Nymphaea hybrida, *from pale pink (shown
here) to deep blue, and throughout the spectrum
of yellows and golds, are good subjects for
sketching, as they are often more accessible than
their wild counterparts (see Fig 25)*

neck are worked first in smooth, sinuous stitching. The ear-tufts are then overlaid in very fine straight stitching, allowing, in places, the brown feathers to peep through – the higher of the two tufts is the less dense. Continuing the donkey-brown radial stitching down the body, switch to river stitch (page 46) where the throat gives way to the breast of the bird and the direction of stitching must change. The rest of the body can then be filled in, the strata subdued by fine directional stitching in white, serving a double purpose; first to soften the contours and second to act as a long ticking stitch to convey the flecks of white on the russet-red down of the belly.

Whether worked on a pale ground, or dark (Plate 35), the water-lily is a beautiful study, its fleshy petals surrounded by four sepals, white above and green beneath, often delicately reflexed (Plate 34), at its centre a mass of buttery-gold stamens. As the colour of the petals is more or less uniform (sometimes flushed with pink as shown in Plate 35) it is important for the sake of reality to differentiate between the upper and lower surfaces of each petal. Logically, the upper should always be paler than the lower, as the light hits it, but it is not always easy to tell from a rough sketch exactly which petal is which – and whether it is a front, sideways or rear view. Use the stamens at the core of the flower as a reference point (see Fig 25). The petals immediately surrounding them are arranged in a cup shape, the outer petals gradually opening into a saucer and finally flat plate.

The leaves are even more attractive. Waxy green above and reddish pink below they lie on the surface of the water on stems up to 9 feet (2.75m) long. They make their way to the surface like fine arrows, finally cresting the water to

PLATE 36 ▷

Scented mayweed (Chamomilla recutita) *has*
*a pronounced scent of apples (*Chamomilla *is*
derived from the Greek 'apples of the ground')
and this is the plant from which a soothing
infusion of chamomile tea can be made. (It is
also used for highlighting fair hair.) Worked on
a black background, the white petals are a
dramatic motif. Contrasting the bolder elements
of this pattern, the delicate scarlet pimpernel
adds a fluid, sinuous design feature. Its
symmetrical leaves and neat round flowers
bring an air of calm to an otherwise hectic
study. Called the 'poor-man's-weatherglass' in
Norfolk, its petals close in dull weather and
fall immediately they are picked. It is seen at
its best just after eight o'clock on sunny summer
mornings between May and August when you
may be able to sketch the new flowers almost
as they open
16 x 23cm (6¼ x 9 inches)

stand briefly above it (Plate 35, top right) and opening out into carpets of gently undulating green, each leaf finely veined with a darker shade. As individual motifs they are excellent for demonstrating the full 360-degree arc of radial work, and well defined reflex stitching, but it is fun to emphasize the watery location of these superb plants by allowing fine stitches of blue to overlap the body of the leaves themselves. These may be worked in floss or twisted threads, or a combination of both, and the technique may also be used to lap over the sepals of the lily. Do not be tempted to put too many of these 'ripples' into the design – they could overwhelm the beautiful simplicity of the plants – but experiment at design stage. It is better not to transfer a drawn line indicating water on to the fabric; decide on the extent of the water while you are actually working the study.

White, red and yellow on black is a vibrant combination. Where the wildflowers in Plate 34 conveyed a hazy, peaceful scene, in Plate 36 (minus the blue forget-me-nots) the colours fuse together to create all the fire and passion of a baking Indian summer. Because of the strength of the individual colours they can be quite few in number – and the design, although spread wide across the fabric, is lightweight. The papery red heads of the poppies are echoed by the scarlet pimpernel – all the other flowers are species of daisy.

In order to become entirely familiar with any plant it is necessary to appreciate its anatomy from every angle. The open-faced mayweed is shown here from the side, back and front revealing the scaly bracts, the pincushion golden centre and its slim profile – a basic anatomy which it shares with the corn marigold (bottom left) and the strangely alien pineapple weed (bottom right).

The origin of the pineapple weed *(Chamomilla suaveolens)* is unknown, although it is thought to have been used medicinally in antiquity, probably in north-east Asia. It was introduced into Britain only in the last quarter of the nineteenth-century, from Oregon in the United States and immediately gained a foothold colonizing farmyards, paths and gateways – in fact any well-trampled ground. What at first appears to be a mass of stamens with fallen petals, is, in fact, the flower head in its prime. The almost spherical yellow dome is made up of tubular florets, too small to be embroidered separately other than by a dense cluster of seed stitches apparently sitting in an 'egg-cup' of whitish-green bracts. A close relative of the scented mayweed, it has an almost identical leaf, deeply divided and growing at intervals along the main stem of the plant.

It is impossible to apply the normal rules of leaf embroidery to a species such as this. There is no obvious centre vein, no broad palmate shape to infill.

◁ *Fig 25*

Simplify your sketch of a water lily to become
familiar with its structure. Block in underside
features, leaving upper surfaces blank. Only
when you are sure of its anatomy is it safe to
attempt a more impressionistic interpretation

Fig 26 △

Grasses. Clockwise from the left: creeping twitch, crested dog's tail, cock's foot and meadow foxtail

PLATE 37 ▷

The ladybird in Plate 36 has made its way into this study also! Seen in greater detail in Plate 7 (page 13) the seven-spot ladybird (Coccinella 7-punctata) is one of the most common of the 40 or so recorded species. In flight the ladybird opens its familiar spotted red wing-cases to reveal long delicate wings which make it a strong flier. Work the wing-cases first, superimposing the spots by the use of studding, then the tiny segmented body. On black, the legs and antennae can be worked either in fine white or gold metallic thread – depending on the desired effect – but the wings must be worked in the narrowest possible gauge of white (or black on a pale ground) upper and lower wings radiating from the body beneath the cases. The short cropped grass at the base of the picture, worked in a 3/1T cotton, softens the line of the rabbit's body, and its feet, barely visible through the grass, are suggested rather than detailed, emphasizing the way in which the rabbit nestles into the undergrowth

19 x 20cm (7½ x 7¾ inches)

Instead, rather irregular jagged stem stitch must be used to capture the ragged, dishevelled qualities of these plants. Where the leaf segments cross the main stem, such as on the mayweed, work right over the top of the more distant feature adding to the three-dimensional effects of the design.

The ox-eye daisy *(Leucanthemum vulgare)*, with its very similar flower (Plate 37), has a fuller-bodied leaf, which can be treated traditionally; radiating from a central vein the stitches slip backwards to an elongated core, light yellow-green above and darker on the side of the shadow line. The flower heads are again shown at a variety of angles, each petal slightly notched at its outer edge.

Unlike the solid-stemmed sedges, grasses have hollow fibrous stems with slender leaf blades and much-simplified flowers. They often have delightful country nicknames: crested dog's tail, cock's foot, meadow foxtail and creeping twitch (Fig 26). In the mid-1700s the meadow cat's tail *(Phleum pratense)*, previously a wild grass of low lying water meadows, became a major hay crop when American agriculturalist Timothy Hanson had the sub-species *pratense* named after him. His theory that it could be excellent cattle fodder was proved in the colonies, the crop was reintroduced to Britain and 'Timothy' remains a popular harvested hay. It is shown in Plate 37.

The long, sinuous leaves reflex and coil so intricately that it is important to remember which is the upper and which the lower surface (here your sketch can help) and to differentiate the two by colouring. Snake stitch allows the fields of the blade to be infilled smoothly without fighting the curve (see Appendix A) and the base of each leaf curls around the stem of the grass in a sheath, the stitches disappearing down a well-like funnel. The flowers of many grasses, including these, are composed of dozens of 'spikelets' , each of which contains a single floret and numerous stamens. The long, sausage-shaped body of the flower can be embroidered as a mass of oval spikelets (each delicately shadow lined) and then overlaid with a dusting of fine seed stitches, purplish-brown and lightening to gold before they are borne away on the wind.

Rabbits were not introduced into Britain until the twelfth century – and not until the reign of Elizabeth I did they escape close captivity and become naturalized wild residents. In terms of embroidery even a baby rabbit is a 'large animal' and must be worked in solid, stocky *opus plumarium* with no hint of background fabric showing through the stitching. Highly prized by the Normans (hence their bringing it to Britain) rabbit fur is by no means a uniform shade: dark and light shades of brown and grey mingle throughout, and here it may be useful to create your own threads. With fine floss, try forming a 3/1 or 4/1F comprising two grey and one or two brown strands. Work the upper body in this, and as you move down the animal's flank vary the components – darkening the fur by using only one grey stand and more brown. Reverse the process as you approach the light chest area, gradually incorporating more grey and then white in your mixed thread. By using fine strands you can create an almost infinite variety of thread colours.

PLATE 38 ▷

The Adonis blue (Lysandra bellargus) *is distinguishable from all other blue butterflies by the chequered black and white band around the edges of its wings. The male is a vivid blue – hence its naming after Adonis the god of masculine beauty. The underside of the wing is a mass of white, orange and black studding.*

If a butterfly is to be shown alighted on a flower or leaf, work the body of the insect first, and then the leaf around it. The fine spindly legs may then be worked over the top of the leaf

9.5 x 9.5cm (3¾ x 3¾ inches)

A COOLING DRAUGHT

Animals and insects make odd alliances, the simplicity of the food chain is not the only link between species, and the humble rabbit has in places helped the survival of one of Britain's rarest and most beautiful butterflies, the Adonis blue. Largely dependent upon wildflowers which prefer open grassy slopes and wide headlands, intensive ploughing and the destruction of common land has drastically reduced their numbers. Where they survive, it is often thanks to the close cropping of grass by rabbits and where rabbits decline the Adonis blues have little chance of maintaining their perilous foothold.

A plant which could be particularly attractive to the Adonis blue in the wild, and which is also widely cultivated as animal fodder, is the red clover *(Trifolium pratense)*. Its delicate scent also attracts other long-tongued insects, in particular bees which are strong enough to force the lips of the florets apart and gain access to the nectar.

The structure of the clover florets is extraordinary. The upper and lower petals surround a third, which in turn protects the stamens. For the embroiderer, the flower head appears to be a red-purple pom-pon arising from a pair of flattened leaves at the end of each stem. Each floret, individually shadow lined, is worked in a pale shade, the lower petal superimposed by a short shooting stitch of darker purple, more visible towards the base of the flower head, and disappearing as the crown of the flower is approached. The leaves are extremely attractive: each is formed of three narrow pointed leaflets bearing a pale V-shaped band. Work the pale-green stem and veins of the leaves first in a fairly short stem stitch, and then each side of the leaflets in turn, pale above and darker beneath. The 'V' marking must appear distinct and may be worked in the same pale green as the vein, shooting radial stitches out over the existing embroidery.

Clover honey was particularly prized for making mead (an alcoholic brew of fermented honey) and the flowers of the red clover can be made into a potent country wine. Many shrubs and herbs were used to slake man's thirst for alcohol, whether through wine, beer or spirits, and what began as a housewife's chore became a cottage industry and finally big business. Many buildings remain in the countryside which owe their origins to the brewing industry and, like barns, many have been converted into beautiful homes. Plate 39 shows an old malt-house. Left to fall into decay after its working days were past it has been restored to its rightful place as an important feature of the changing face of rural England.

Pantiles, slates, brick, flint and wood are all part of this attractive building. We have discussed how to achieve the effect of brick and flint – but the variation in angles of the roofs and the building materials used requires further investigation. The red pantiles on the nearest roof are difficult to see as the pitch is so steep; they are suggested merely by colouring, as are the slates on the roof behind. The shallow curve of the roof facing, however, can be made out. Using a matt thread (at least 2/1T) work long stitches from the apex of the roof to the eaves. Then work bold laddering, interweaving at least five or six threads at a time with a single horizontal thread. This creates a roughly chequerboard effect. To create a 'lowlight' on the edges of the slates, work a darker thread through the laddering, at the angle of the roof's pitch, and always to the same side of each chequer. The order of this working is shown in Fig 27. The stitches will merge slightly, softening the effect and giving the impression of a very solid structure. The wood above the main flintwork wall is, by contrast, worked in a floss thread – a twisted thread would have been dull and overpowering. On the actual building, the wood had been treated and was a dark grey-brown. The unconventional use of a floss in long horizontal bands means that this dour colour is lifted by the light catching the shine of the thread.

Fig 27 ▷
Work straight stitching at the angle of the pitch (1), and then ladder through the existing embroidery at the angle shown by the hatched line (2). Finally, lay a second laddered line to one side of the pitch line as indicated at (3). Repeat the process, if necessary, over dormer windows etc

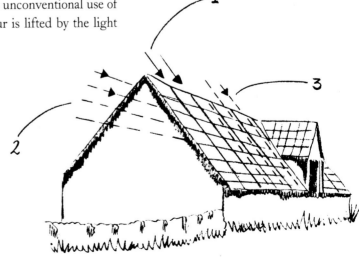

HELEN
STEVENS

CHAPTER FOUR

BROADS, FENS AND WATERWAYS

*At last he came to a bank of beautiful
shrubs; whitebeam with its great silver backed
leaves, and mountain ash, and oak with great
beds of crown ferns and wood sedge; while
through the shrubs he could see the stream
sparkling ... and a neat pretty cottage*

The Water Babies
Charles Kingsley

HELEN
STEVENS

◁ *PLATE 48 (see also page 84)*

MESSING ABOUT ON THE RIVER

Blue is the colour of tranquillity, of long languid days lazily gazing at the water and counting its shades from ice-blue to aquamarine, from the baby-blue of the water forget-me-nots to the purple bells of the comfrey and spikes of water violets. Water itself, of course, is colourless: it is only the reflection of sky and landscape which gives it an appearance of colour, and this is a clue as to why pictures containing large expanses of water can be doubly successful, capturing not only scenery but also atmosphere.

Plate 40 was inspired by a scene in north Devon. A broad stream ran beneath a pack bridge carrying a carters' track from one bank to the other. The track continued past a cottage, along the side of the river, skirted shrubs and plants and finally meandered away from the water, between fields and hedges. A sudden noise startled a pheasant from the undergrowth and simultaneously a pair of mallards winged over the water. I wanted to recreate that day just as I saw and felt it, but as we have discussed before, embroidery is an art which requires careful planning before a needle can be threaded or a stitch can be taken.

A photograph of this scene would be conveniently bounded by the dimensions of the image – the river would run off the edge of the picture, the fields would be cut off by its border and the sky would meet the horizon, filling the entire field of the study. Embroidery must evoke and frame the scene without relying upon unnaturally straight lines to hold the picture in place. The fact that

Fig 28 ▷
The central feature of a study is important but it is also essential to define the limits of the picture. The partridge and chicks, while adding extra interest to the sketch, 'round off' the foreground, the wildflowers to the right frame the work and the skyline echoes the curve of the bridge

Detail of Plate 40. As a thatch ages, it loses its flaxen gold colouring and matures to an attractive grey-brown. Etching and dashing make up the body of the cottage, the daub and wattle walls sugar brown. Tiny reflections of light appear at the bottom left-hand corner of each window pane, worked in ice-blue floss silk and laid over matt 2/1T black thread.

The pheasant (Phasianus colchicus) is not a native of Britain, but was introduced from the Caucasus in the Middle Ages for the sweetness of its meat. A second strain was brought from China in the seventeenth century — and these, unlike the bird featured here, can be distinguished by the white ring around their necks. Chinese embroideries featuring the pheasant date back centuries, and Mary Queen of Scots incorporated it in the famous Marian Hangings
Width of detail shown 11cm (4¼ inches)

the water reflects the blue of the sky illustrates that the sky is blue! A mass of stitching to create the sky itself would simply detract from the rest of the study. The river sweeps first to the right, and then gently curves away to the left. This movement is indicated by the final stratum of straight stitches disappearing behind the roses framing the bottom left of the picture. As the pheasant rises, it marks the boundary of the subject's specific interest to the top right (Plate 41), while the tree (top left), separates the middle distance and true background. Finally, the tall comfrey (bottom right) disguises the edge of the track. These features define the limits of the study. Within them, the eye may be drawn into fine details, or led from one motif to the next by broad, bold stitching, but with these boundaries set, we know 'where to stop'.

Look back at Plates 30 and 39 to see how this principle has been applied to those landscapes. In your own sketchbook, try to remember to pick out features which will 'frame' your studies at this preliminary stage (see Fig 28), and it will make life easier at the drawing board. When you transfer your final design, include these defining elements in some detail, but where the blending edge (Fig 29) of water or grass merges into the background fabric, omit the suggested line; it is better to make the final decision as to the limit of this stitching when embroidery is actually underway.

Although shown only in the distance, the pack bridge in Plate 40 is the central element and 'scene setter' of this study. It emerges boldly from the water,

Fig 29 ▽

A simple motif such as the water violet should be transferred on to the fabric without an indication of the water below. Using the sketch as reference if necessary, the water should be added freehand in straight stitching when the rest of the design has been worked

HELEN
STEVENS

◁ *PLATE 40*
'River Cottage'. Many riverside trees and
plants have a blue-green or silvery tinge to
their foliage which adds to the cool, relaxed
quality of an embroidered waterscape. The
leaves of the crack willow (Salix fragilis)*, left,*
are shiny green above and silver-grey below,
the familiar shape of the pollarded tree, round
and compact as it leans over the water at a
crazy angle. On the opposite bank the osier
*(*Salix viminalis)*, also a willow, is a shrub*
rather than a tree, coppiced to produce 'withies'
for basket-making. These gentle, rounded
shapes create a pleasing contrast with the spikes
of wildflowers in the foreground, yellow
loosestrife (Lysimachia vulgaris) *and water*
violets (Hottonia palustris) *growing,*
respectively, on the bank and in the water
31 x 27cm (12¼ x 10½ inches)

PLATE 42 ▷

Victorian waterside beggars and ne'er-do-wells
collected river limpet shells, filled them with
the sap of the lesser spearwort (Ranunculus
flammula), and bound them to their bodies to
raise sores – and money from canal traders –
just as their medieval counterparts preyed upon
early pilgrims. Purple loosestrife (Lythrum
salicaria) takes its Latin name from the
willow-like properties of the plant. Both favour
clean flowing waters, especially at the edges of
water meadows. Remember when you make
sketches of wildflowers that their 'habits' are as
important as their physical appearance. The
fluid, fragile stalks of the spearwort are in
direct contrast to the thrusting, upright stem of
the loosestrife. Try to make a flowing, single
curve for the former which will transfer in an
unbroken arc, and rough out the acute
triangular form of the loosestrife before fleshing
it out with detail
15 x 26cm (5¾ x 10 inches)

Fig 30 △

Centrally radiating plants in the middle
distance catch the light, and if positioned
alongside matt features, such as a rock, can be
particularly effective

. . . .

the undersides of its arches strongly shadowed by etching, the masonry itself in firm dot stitching. Beneath each pier the water is shadowed, beyond it can just be seen emerging into the sunlight.

At all times the water is the key to the conditions within the study. Just as the darker shades close to the bank and beneath overhanging shrubs and water plants indicate that it is shadowed in these places, so the pale ice-blue at the centre of the stream tells us that the sun is shining, an effect enhanced by working centrally radiating plants, such as the moor grass, bottom centre, which catches the natural light outside the picture (see Fig 30).

A tall, striking plant such as the Russian comfrey *(Symphytum × uplandicum)* not only makes an attractive feature in the middle distance, where it can be blended with its natural surroundings by the simple method of including a few blades of grass growing around its base in long, straight, upright stitches, but may also be chosen as one of the plants to 'bring forward' into the foremost framing element (bottom left). By using a plant already incorporated elsewhere in the study a sense of continuity is effected. The bell-shaped flowers and buds nod from a coiled stem, bright green leaves growing in pairs. The same coiled motif is reflected in the tufted forget-me-not *(Myosotis laxa ssp caespitosa)*. This beautiful plant is a joy, as on each stem the flowers vary in colour – from deep pink as small buds, through paler pink as the bud opens and into blue and yellow in the fully opened flower.

Sometimes, a plant explored as a distant motif can inspire a larger, close up study in its own right. The purple loosestrife growing beside the water in Plate 40 is shown in greater detail in Plate 42. This regal plant is rich in tannins and its juice has been used as an alternative to oak bark extract for the purposes of tanning and dying. The flowers are set in whorls around the stem of the plant, and to be embroidered convincingly it is necessary to show the flowers from all angles. The lowest whorl in this study is the best example. While at least one of the flowers is shown facing the viewer, others are shown in profile, or from the rear. The back of the petals are veined with a darker purple, and by emphasizing this the structure of the plant is more easily shown. The leaves have no stalks – simple and ovate in form they are set in whorls of three towards the base of the plant and in pairs higher up. Working on black, the colours are particularly spectacular, and may be further highlighted by the addition of another, simpler plant in contrast. The lesser spearwort is really no more than a common buttercup with narrow spear-like leaves – hence its everyday name. As a motif it is a perfect foil for more complicated plants, its only unusual feature being its fruiting head. This globe-shaped body is made up of a number of small ovate seeds, worked closely together as groups of short straight stitches separated by narrow voiding lines. Remember that if you use a finer thread your voiding line can become proportionately more delicate, as the width of the void should be approximately the same as the gauge of your thread.

Plate 41 shows the flustered, flapping flight of the pheasant as it rises into

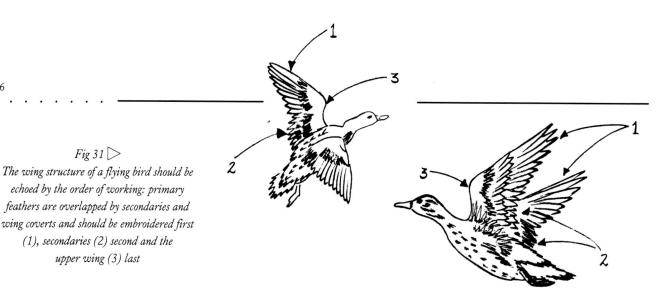

Fig 31 ▷
The wing structure of a flying bird should be echoed by the order of working: primary feathers are overlapped by secondaries and wing coverts and should be embroidered first (1), secondaries (2) second and the upper wing (3) last

PLATE 43 △
Detail of Plate 40. Mallards (Anas platyrhynchos) *are the most familiar species of duck in both town and country, and are generally so trusting that the close proximity of a struggling artist will not bother them in the slightest. Take advantage of their relaxed attitude to get near enough to examine their feathers – this is where* opus plumarium *(feather work) gets its name. As the shades and colours of the feathers merge and blend they demonstrate exactly the effects we often try to achieve*
Actual size of largest duck:
4cm (1½ inches)

· · · · · · · · ·

the air. Pheasants always seem to prefer taking to their heels rather than taking to the air (indeed, they are not capable of long-distance flight), but when startled they can rise quickly and steeply. Plate 43 homes in on the deliberate, muscle-pumping flight of the ducks. Where birds are included in the middle or far distance of a large picture, because the finest details must be omitted for reasons of scale, it is important to capture the 'essence' of a bird as well as its most characteristic outline and colouring.

Obviously, you must work in a finer thread than has been used for foreground details, but certain rules still apply – primarily the shadow stitching. This, if anything, is even more important during miniaturization as it creates a bold outline – and often it is the fleeting silhouette of a bird which catches the eye in reality. Rationalize the bird's primary features. In the pheasant, these include the long train of the tail feathers, the backward sweep of the wings (loose feathered, they allow light through the quills) and the unmistakable jaunty set of the crest. Apart from the darker head and neck, and the distinctive red cheek-patches, the bird's colouring is fairly uniform gold-brown. The markings, which in close up would be worked in Dalmatian dog, are clearly too small here to use that technique. They are superimposed by studding and laddering. The final effect is of a speckled, well-camouflaged bird. By very loosely echoing the outline of wing and tail in the termination of the landscape stitching, and by positioning its body below the line of the horizon, the bird is firmly placed in the semi-foreground, and its scale is determined as correct in relation to the rest of the picture.

The ducks are altogether more colourful, and their sunlit flight a more active, positive affair. Again, the overall silhouette is important, but with some dozen or more species of duck relatively common the essential mallard characteristics must be analysed. The yellow bill, orange feet and distinctive white collar of the male give away his identity immediately – the female is dull by comparison though her stocky undercarriage and yellow bill accurately place her at his side! Ducks need strong wings to bear their dense bodyweight, and each primary feather should be carefully outlined and worked individually. The line of the wing coverts should then be worked slightly overlapping the primaries, and finally the secondaries (the order of working similar to a full-sized study). This system works for both the upper and lower sides of the wings (see Fig 31).

A BROADER CANVAS

Many habitats which we now cherish and protect as valuable wildlife sanctuaries and remnants of our past are, in fact, not at all what nature intended. The Norfolk Broads, formed by cutting and dredging; the Cambridgeshire and Lincolnshire Fens, maintained for centuries as a source of peat to heat local homes; canals, once valuable trade links and now chiefly the haunts of pleasure craft; all are man-made marks on the natural countryside.

The high, wide arch of the East Anglian sky is seen nowhere to better effect than in the Broads. Distant clumps and islands of trees break the monotony of sky meeting water, while low-growing grasses, sedges and reeds provide shelter for birds and insects. In a landscape of extremes, unusual dimensions and new ways of conveying now-familiar features, such as distant trees, can create an exciting fresh stimulus.

The broad expanse of water in Plate 44 has been worked similarly to the river in Plate 40, in bold straight, horizontal stitches, positioned close together – the thread in this case a fine 2/1 T. Be brave in your stitching – if your fabric has been correctly mounted in its embroidery frame (see Appendix B) it should be taut enough to support stitches up to 5cm (2 inches) long. It should be possible to work each field of colour in a single width of stitching. In an open landscape such as this there are very few features hanging over the water (where the low vegetation meets the water a darker shade is still effective), but it is still important to vary the shades of blue, both to break up the monotony of colour and to indicate differences in water depth. In the right-hand foreground the deeper blue suggests that the water is lapping into a shallower inlet.

The emphasis on straight stitching is echoed in the distant trees. Across any flat landscape, and waterscapes in particular, distances can be deceptive. What appears to be only a long stone's throw away may in fact be a mile or more. It would be incorrect to pretend that individual branches, let alone leaves, could be made out at these distances and so we must find a new approach. Find a horizon where a substantial number of massed trees meet the sky and study it. Make a rough sketch of what you actually see (not what you think you see!), as shown in Fig 32. The massed foliage of lower trees and shrubs bubble up into the taller elements, colours and density vary, but from this distant perspective few

Fig 32 $\bigtriangledown$

Look at distant trees clumped together on the horizon. They are a jumble of shapes, all essentially thrusting upwards, and can be worked in straight perpendicular stitching with voiding between the planes. The ground, by contrast, is worked in horizontal straight stitching

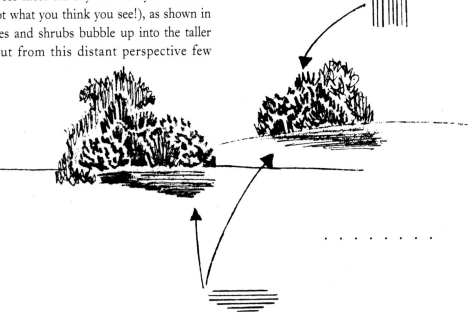

individual features are identifiable. At transfer stage, reproduce only the outlines of these nebulous shapes, and embroider them in straight upright stitches, dividing between bushes, shrubs and trees with voiding lines. Usually colours will appear dull- or even bluish-green as far distances tend to deaden colour. You may also use a variety of differently textured though roughly similarly gauged threads.

Just as the distant grasses in Plate 31 were worked in fine upright stitching to contrast the horizontal meadowlands, all the plant growth in this study is upright. From the far distant reed-beds sweeping away to the tree-line (here the uprights are barely more than dot stitches) to the rushes and reeds of the foreground inlet (detail, Plate 45) they are gradually built up, becoming longer and more dense as they surround other features, such as a clump of wildflowers (willowherb), and intermingle with each other. It is clearly impossible to work every stitch as an identifiable plant. Build up the impression of swaying long-leaved ground cover and allow it to be highlighted by the odd reed-head and

broader-leaved plant which should be worked in advance of the encroaching straight stitches and then softly blended into the whole (see Fig 33).

Just as before, lively interest has been added to this study by the movement of middle-distance birds. The languid, slow-flapping flight of the heron (*Ardea cinerea*) defines the upper limit of the study, its long neck drawn back into its body, legs extended, worked in the same semi-detail already explored. In the inlet the great-crested grebe elegantly glides through the water, mirrored by its own reflection. In Plate 45 it is possible to study the reflection in detail. The rippling water breaks down any solid outline into a series of straight stitches, roughly echoing the outline of the bird above, in a dull brown-grey interspersed with blue. Work the bird and its reflection before the surrounding water: a minimal shadow line (the reflected light from the water will make it largely unnecessary) is aided by a voided outline separating the bird from its surroundings.

Plate 46 is composed from a variety of broadland elements brought together

PLATE 44 △

This unusually wide design, fairly shallow from top to bottom, reflects the open, unspoilt face of the Norfolk Broads. The huge arc of the East Anglian sky is suggested by reflection rather than by inclusion, as is the breeze by the blowing seeds of the willowherb to the left. The scope of the picture is bounded by this plant and the wild roses to the right. A large canvas such as this requires careful mounting and framing (see Appendix B), and has been designed to 'run off' the canvas to the right where the distant trees end abruptly 62.5 x 23.0cm (24½ x 9 inches)

. . . .

PLATE 45 ▷

Detail of Plate 44. The great-crested grebe (Podiceps cristatus) *was almost wiped out during the last century when the fashion for ladies' grebe-feather hats and the passion for feather collage and 'embroidery' reduced their numbers almost to the point of extinction. Fortunately, they are now protected and a healthy population exists. The willowherb in the foreground of Plate 44 has been echoed in the middle distance as shown here. Its essential elements have been extrapolated – tall, spear-like growth, short leaves, pink flowers with yellow core – just enough information to identify it and lead the eye deeper into the picture*

Fig 33 ▽

In the middle distance it is impossible to define every leaf and blade of grass. Work certain features first, such as reed heads, lilies, rocks, etc, and roughly sketch in the surrounding foliage. Repeat this order of working in your embroidery. Define certain elements and then build up impressionistic straight stitches (both grasses and the water) around them

in detail. The reed bunting *(Emberiza schoeniclus)* is to waterways what the house sparrow is to city parks. Its cheeky, chirruping song and characteristic tail-flick as it flits from one clump of grasses to the next identifies this common British resident, whose nest sites not only include reed-beds and riversides but also sewage farms! It eats mainly seed and grain, but in the summer and during the breeding season insects and caterpillars may be taken.

Of all the stages of a butterfly's life, it is at its most vulnerable as a caterpillar, and many insects attempt to protect themselves not by camouflage, but by warning off predators. The caterpillar of the swallowtail butterfly, shown here on its only food plant the milk parsley, displays a pair of bright orange horns and gives off a smell of ripe pineapples. Its lumpy, segmented body is bright green,

PLATE 46

With the exception of the dragonfly and its prey (low-level activity), all the elements in this study lead the eye upwards. Although they are broadly spaced the canvas feels full of activity as each element leads on to the next. The whip-like upper stems of the milk parsley are smoothly worked in stem stitch, taking care always to follow rather than 'fight' the curve. Where the stems become straighter and sturdier the stem stitch evolves into a broad, infilling technique. It is always easier to work towards the shadow line, so allow your stitches to fall smoothly down towards the base of the plant (see Fig 34)

19 x 34.5cm (7½ x 13½ inches)

HELEN STEVENS

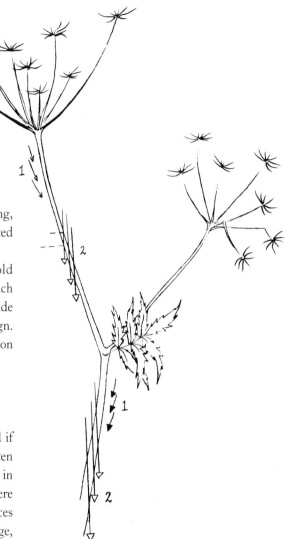

Fig. 34 ▷

Milk parsley (like other members of its family) has strong, straight lower stems and gently curving upper stalks. Remember not to 'fight the curve' when attempting these shapes. Curving lines should be worked in stem stitch (remember the shadow line first). The straight stems should be shadowed with stem stitch in the direction shown by the black arrows (1) and infilled with straight stitching as indicated by the open arrows (2)

with red and black markings, too small for any technique other than studding, which should be superimposed over a base of infill stitching, each segment treated separately, and appropriately shadow lined.

The gatekeeper *(Pyronia tithonus)*, is an unassuming brown and gold butterfly whose colours echo those of the reed bunting. In a composite study such as this, try to find certain elements which link the picture together. There is a wide diversity of colour here, scattered across the fabric in a lively, dancing design. Without some continuity it might be in danger of becoming a random collection of motifs.

BEAUTY ABOVE, BEAST BELOW

During the Dark and Middle Ages, fens and meres were places to be avoided if possible. Not only were they the haunts of outlaws and bandits, but were often thought to harbour supernatural terrors. The monster Grendel and his mother in the epic *Beowulf* were to be found along '. . . a dangerous fen path, where the mere stands', and the will-o'-the-wisp, a strange phosphorescent light which dances over marshy waters, lured many an unwary explorer to his death. The strange, other-worldliness of the undrained Fens survives in very few places now, as land has been made safe for agriculture, but where undisturbed marshes and bogs exist one of the true exotic beauties of the countryside may still be found.

The unattractively named bogbean *(Menyanthes trifoliata)* is a fairy-tale plant of pale pink featherlike flowers and handsome bright-green leaves (Plate 47). The

◁ *PLATE 47*

Not only beautiful but beneficial, the bogbean was used to purify the blood, cure scurvy, and as a general tonic – not least as a flavouring for home-brewed beer. The large, fleshy leaves are effectively worked in contrasting shades of green, their plain ovate form a perfect foil for the elaborate flowers.

Working honeycomb stitch on a black ground requires the same fine gauge of thread as on a pale fabric – but white shows up better than a colour. If you want to add a coloured sheen, separate a strand of coloured cellophane from a blending filament and overlay the honeycomb stitching with fine radial work

15 x 26cm (5¾ x 10 inches)

PLATE 48 ▷

While the kingfisher (Alcedo atthis) *waits patiently above the water to spot a passing fish, below the surface an alien world goes about its business. Many water plants have two forms of leaf structure: the common water-crowfoot* (Ranunculus aquatilis) *has flat open leaves which crest the water and fine, grasslike submerged leaflets. The skullcap* (Scutellaria galericulata) *with its pretty blue flowers may either grow directly from the water or on the river bank; in the former case its rigid stem is an ideal route to the world above for the downy emerald nymph as it clambers upwards prior to emerging into its shimmering adult form.*

Towards the bottom left the lesser water boatman (Corixa) *pursues the still tinier* Daphnia *or water fleas, himself the object of the stickleback's attention. Shimmering water effects are created by separating the cellophane strand from a blending filament and working long, straight horizontal stitches. Low level water weeds are worked in floating stitch, and the fish in laddering and couching (see* The Embroiderer's Countryside*). Seed beads are massed together to suggest water-polished pebbles, while simple* opus plumarium, *stem and straight stitching complete the other elements of the design*

tubular buds emerge from pink-tinged sepals and then burst open revealing five ethereal petals fringed with white, cottony hairs. The basic flower head should be worked first, paying particular attention to the directional sweep of the radial stitching as it emerges from the throat, which should be shadowed in dark grey. Then, using a single strand of fine thread, and strictly following the direction of the main stitching, overlay a fine straight feathering of stitches, projecting beyond the original strata.

The downy emerald dragonfly *(Cordulia aenea)* is a darter common to both still and flowing waters. Its metallic green head and thorax and deep russet-bronze abdomen make it one of the most easily identifiable dragonflies – especially as it spends much of its time clinging to plants, sallying forth to catch prey in flight only when it cannot find a less agile meal. The transformation from hideous nymph into beautiful adult is one of nature's most extraordinary feats. It survives as a nymph (larva) for two years underwater, before climbing up the stem of a plant, shedding its skin and living for a brief span as an imago. Beneath the surface of the water, however, even the ugly nymph can provide inspiration. Here in a silver-washed world the imagination can run riot. Floating embroidery, tiny couched bubbles, swirls and eddies of reflected light from the world above combine in a fantasia of colour and movement.

CHAPTER FIVE

THE DAPPLED SHADE

They were standing in the shade of hazel bushes. The sunlight, filtering through innumerable leaves, was still hot on their faces. In a ragged hedge the boughs of the elm trees swayed just perceptibly in the breeze, and their leaves stirred faintly in dense masses like women's hair.

Nineteen Eighty-Four
George Orwell

HELEN
STEVENS

◁ *PLATE 49 (Also cover picture)*
'The Laundress's Cottage'. The old sundial,
festooned with creeper, is worked in etching
and dashing. A rounded, bellied shape such as
this requires careful analysis for the purposes of
shadowing or it will appear flat and
uninteresting (see Fig 36)
Embroidery shown life size:
23.5 x 30cm (9¼ x 11¾ inches)

In a small Suffolk village, until about 20 years ago, a daub-and-wattle cottage clung tenaciously to existence, its walls festooned with the remnants of once-cultivated climbing plants, its garden an overgrown tangle of country perennials, lupins, hollyhocks and geraniums. In its hedge, plum trees weighed heavy with fruit in the autumn and every winter the frost destroyed a little more of its mossy thatch. Then, quite suddenly, it was gone, replaced by a 'spacious, well-appointed bungalow', as the estate agent's particulars read.

Woodbine Cottage had escaped the renovator's attention: like its last occupant it disappeared into oblivion leaving only faint clues to its former importance in village hierarchy, for it had once been the Laundress's cottage,

PLATE 50 ▷
Detail of Plate 49. Long, straight diagonal
dashing has been used to create the thatch, the
angle changing subtly as it approaches the
facing wall and then sweeps away to the right.
This was worked initially in the primary
'straw' coloured cotton, and then darker
strands and mossy green threads were
interspersed at the eaves. A 2/1T silk was
added at the apex of the roof to give the
appearance of weathering
Detail shown: 13 x 15.5cm (5 x 6 inches)

where a generation of local gentry had entrusted their dirty linens to the washerwoman, to be returned washed, pressed, clear-starched and sweet smelling. In the remnants of its garden the raw materials of her trade survived for some time, and still appear sporadically in adjoining hedges and ditches, where, close shadowed by trees, they have not been disturbed by building or agriculture. After a little detective work, I was inspired to recreate the cottage and its surroundings (Plate 49 and cover picture).

Woodbine is the country name for honeysuckle, which still riots around local hedgerows. Its clockwise spiralling stems coil themselves so tightly around trees and saplings that it can actually deform its host into curious 'barley sugar' twists, and the vigour with which it invaded its namesake's thatch contributed significantly to its final downfall. Even so, it must once have been a pretty sight to see it trained through the climbing roses up to the chimney stack and beyond, the roses, chocolate-box fashion, rambling around the eaves, with other climbers, clematis and convolvulus clinging together in great swags of colour.

The cottage is worked from memory – spiced with imagination! I know that the thatch was shallow-pitched and ragged, that the door had peeling remnants of greenish-blue paint with three stone steps leading down to the path (Plate 50). Were there once terracotta pots containing herbs and sweet violets and white-framed, leaded windows? I like to think so.

This cottage is worked on a larger scale than any we have yet attempted. It means that more detail can be included – but also presents structural problems. Where we could get away with impressionistic etching and dashing on the river cottage, here we must seriously consider texture, light and shade. For the plasterwork, beams and their attendant shadows, 3/1T silk has been used. For the thatch, a softer thread seemed desirable, one which would blend more softly into darker shades for shadowing, and merge smoothly into mossy greens. After some experimentation, a 2/1T cotton was used (actually a single strand from a six-stranded embroidery cotton). Where the ragged eaves of the thatch overhang the beams this variance of texture creates a three-dimensional effect.

Very little etching has been used. Hard shadows would be inappropriate. Instead, the dark-brown wooden beams were completed in dashing stitch and their uneven outlines 'lowlighted' by an occasional black stitch. The plasterwork was then dashed into position, a darker shade used beneath the main window and above the lower angles of the beams – as though water had gathered and seeped into the plasterwork, gradually deepening its colour.

To emphasize the windows a contrast was needed to the grainy plasterwork. The frames are worked in floss silk, in imitation of gloss paint, and I wanted to create the impression of something being *inside* the building. Before filling in the field of the window with fine ice-blue silk, a few strands of red were laid down on either side, the blue then interspersed and blocked in. Over this was laid, crisscrossed, fine black threads forming the leaded panes (see Fig 35). The effect is of curtains behind the glass, indistinct and yet definitely present.

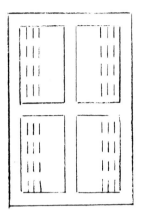

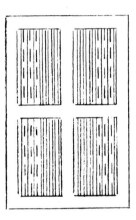

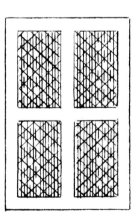

Fig 35 △
Window panes with 'something inside'!
(Top) Work a few perpendicular lines
in a fairly bright colour as indicated by the
hatched line.
(Centre) Intersperse and infill with pale blue.
(Bottom) Overlay black thread lattice-fashion
to complete the window

Fig 36 △

The round-bellied shape of the sundial requires
careful shadowing.

(Top) Transfer the basic outline of the sundial.
(Centre) Shadow line as usual and etch in
deeper shadows in black and dark grey.
(Bottom) Superimpose foliage coiled around the
belly and neck and emerging at the top, and
suggest the long grasses around the foot of the
sundial. Use floss thread for the 'living'
elements to contrast the matt surface of the stone

The chimney stack is worked in dotting, red brick shades light to one side and then deepening on the shaded side of the building, and the stone steps below the door are in similar technique with the addition of a distinct area of etching where the steep risers are in shadow.

Garden flowers may be miniaturized by identifying and simplifying their essential characteristics in the same way as wildflowers. The rambling roses, morning glory and honeysuckle are not only recognizable by the colour and shape of their flowers, but also the shades of their greenery – light and dark blue-green for the roses, typically yellow-green convolvulus leaves and softer, true greens for the honeysuckle. The flowers of all three are used as a framework for the full study, linking and harmonizing shapes and shades. Hollyhocks stand window-high by the long wall, and a lupin, star leafed with deep shell-pink flower spikes, is to the right of the door.

Disguised as a washerwoman after his escape from prison, Mr Toad of Toad Hall thought, in desperation, 'If it comes to that, I suppose any fool can *wash*'. He was, of course, wrong and the herbs and plants, once gathered from the wayside and then more conveniently cultivated, bear witness to the complicated process of fine laundering before the advent of fabric conditioners and spray starch. The roots of common valerian, *Valeriana officinalis* (Plate 51), were dried and laid among bed linen while it was aired to keep it fresh and sweet smelling. This had a double purpose – not only was the fragrance considered pleasant, but it had a sedative quality which induced sound sleep. Together with a fine, showy collection of lords and ladies *(Arum maculatum)*, whose roots were boiled to produce starch for collars and cuffs, it still grows beneath the old plum trees.

Both these plants are fascinating studies for embroidery – in form so different, in colour so similar. Valerian is an umbellifor (all the flower stalks are of the same length, arising from the same point), its delicate pink flowers and deeper pink buds opening slowly to reveal golden yellow stamens. The strong straight stem may be worked similarly to that in Plate 46, and the leaves too, bear a resemblance to the foliage of the milk parsley, divided into pairs of opposite leaflets, each deeply toothed.

The 'lords and ladies' presents us with a form unlike any other we have yet attempted. This strangely shaped flower was, in the Middle Ages, connected with the act of love-making, for obvious visual reasons, the purple-brown spadix swelling rapidly once the flower is fully open, embraced by a yellow-green adapted leaf, or spathe. The spathe is shot through with pink and purple and deeply shadowed as it narrows into a waisted throat. Begin the study with a careful analysis of where the shadow line should occur. The spathe falls forward like a monk's cowl and should be outlined towards the tip, along the fold and downwards to the throat. Work the spadix next, in very fine seed stitch, blending a darker shade into the work as it approaches the grey shadowed area at the top of the throat. Then work the inside of the spathe, in radial *opus plumarium*. Use a 3/1F thread which will allow colours to be blended gradually, first 3 green, then 2

◁ *PLATE 51*
The wood warbler (Phylloscopus sibilatrix)
*is fond of the shady coverts favoured by
woodland plants where its presence is given
away by a glorious, trilling song. Head thrown
back and wings held low is a typical pose. The
open beak retains its central function as the
'core' of the radial stitching – if anything it
makes the strata easier to work, as the angle of
the stitching radiates less acutely in its first few
rows. This applies also to the wren in Plate 54*
15.5 x 28cm (6 x 11 inches)

PLATE 52 △
*Plate 51 shows this study lit correctly: the
broad head of the lords and ladies appears
concave and three-dimensional. Incorrect
lighting (in this case from the left) results in a
flat, lifeless effect: the spadix does not stand out
against the spathe and the voiding appears too
stark. The smooth blending of the 3/1F silk is
destroyed. Try to light work, when hung, from
a similar angle to that used during embroidery*

PLATE 53 ▷

Campanula rotundifolia, harebell in England, is the 'bluebell of Scotland'. Like the lords and ladies, its bell-shaped flowers require careful lighting if all your expert directional stitching it to be fully appreciated. This study is lit from the top right. The small tortoiseshell butterfly is equally at home in gardens, hedgerows and woodland. By choosing a butterfly whose wings contain the same blue colouring as the harebell, a delightful harmony can be created in even a small embroidered study

9 x 9.5cm (3½ x 3¾ inches)

PLATE 54 ▷

Plate 33 and Fig 22 illustrate the importance of 'focusing' the eyes of a bird or animal. Here, the attention of the hedgehog is firmly directed toward the harvestman. Beads drawn from the highlight of the eyes converge upon its body. Above, the wren is seen in profile, its interest centred upon the gnat caught in the spider's web. The highlight of the eye is in a forward position, but more importantly, the open beak may be used to gauge where the fly should be located. Calculate roughly the angle formed between the upper and lower bill and mirror this outwards. If a feature is placed where the lines meet, this will immediately appear to be the centre of attention (see Fig 39)

29.5 x 24.25cm (11¾ x 9½ inches)

green and 1 pink, 1 green and 2 pink and so on. The back of the spathe, seen when it falls forward, is uniformly green, but the blending process may be repeated at the base of the throat. The fine, broad leaves are arrow-shaped and grow on long stalks only from the base of the plant. Use sweeping fields of radial work to convey their strong, fleshy texture.

The dancing heads of the harebell (Plate 53) bob in a nearby piece of pasture land. 'Witches' thimbles' were, like sweet violets, sometimes scattered between the layers of fine handkerchiefs, lace lappets and silk stockings, as much for their confetti-like prettiness as their delicate odour. Bell-shaped flowers, like the spathe of the lords and ladies, must be shadow lined with particular care and the broad, five-lobed petal tube worked in single-stranded, untwisted thread to convey its tissue-thin, papery quality.

FRUIT AND NUT

In the dappled light and shade of the plum and crab-apple trees, other fruit- and nut-bearing shrubs provide home and food for animals, birds and insects whose lives have gone on unchanged despite the passing of Woodbine Cottage and its occupants. Beneath a canopy of leaves all is shifting light and shadow. Where the sunlight succeeds in penetrating, it seems brighter, like daubs of concentrated colour on a dull canvas. Where shadows persist they seem deeper, darker, almost

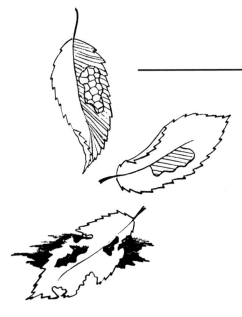

Fig 37 △

Honeycomb stitch, straight, open stitching and shadowing all create different effects to suggest the crumbling structure of dead leaves

tangible. A black background is a perfect foil to capture these effects. Plate 54 is full of activity and movement, sharp contrasts of shape and vivid patches of sunshine.

Techniques which we have explored in other settings, may be used here to recreate unexpected and difficult subjects. We have used honeycomb stitch before only to work the wings of dragonflies, but there are other natural phenomena which call for this cellular effect. Strip away the surface of a leaf, and the veins underneath are revealed. Fallen autumn leaves, or leaves partly eaten by insects often display this effect. Work the main body of the leaf first, leaving a 'hole' within its structure. With a fine thread (in a similar colour) work radial stitches at the same angle as the original work at intervals of about 2mm (⅛ inch) across the open area. When the 'brickwork' stitches pull the radial stitches into the familiar polygon shapes they appear to form a continuous plane leading from and blending into the main body of the leaf (see Fig 37).

The leaf shown is the sweet chestnut *(Castanea sativa)* and beside it hangs the tree's green, spiny-husked fruit. Here, chevron stitch, which we have used before on thistles and teasels, again comes to the rescue. The shrivelled remnants of male catkins are still attached to the base of the husks, worked in seeding stitch. The tiny wren juxtaposed with these elements gives an indication of scale, and these motifs alone would form a fine, small study, though they are equally effective as the lynchpins of a larger embroidery, one branch leading the eye down to the hedgehog (more chevron work) and the other via the spider's web to the enchanter's nightshade *(Circaea lutetiana)*.

Enchanter's nightshade is a willowherb, although unlike other members of its family its seeds are not dispersed by the wind, but by animals and birds. The pale, bell-shaped flowers have a luminous quality amid the shadows in which they are usually found – adding to their supernatural associations. The plant is named for the mythical sorceress Circe, and the Anglo-Saxons called it *aelfthone*, believing it to have powers against spells cast by elves. The flowers droop as they

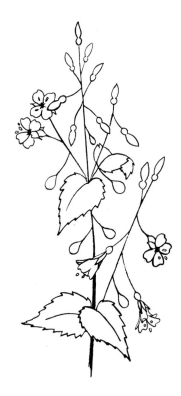

Fig 38 △

Enchanters' nightshade is a complicated, unusual plant, best sketched without shadows or added detail in preparation of your design

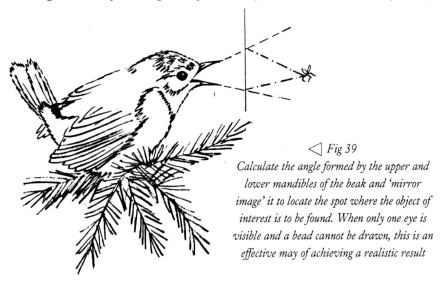

◁ Fig 39

Calculate the angle formed by the upper and lower mandibles of the beak and 'mirror image' it to locate the spot where the object of interest is to be found. When only one eye is visible and a bead cannot be drawn, this is an effective may of achieving a realistic result

◁ *PLATE 55*
There are over a dozen common wild roses
which thrive in hedgerows, each varying
slightly. Here the sweet briar is identifiable in
its hip stage by the persistent sepals which stay
on the fruit far into the autumn and beyond.
The common dormouse was once also called the
hazel dormouse, so synonymous had it become
with its favourite food. In a study such as this,
dominated by golds, green and browns, the
introduction of the bright red hips provides
just enough of a contrast to throw the main
features into relief
16.5 x 16.5cm (6½ x 6½ inches)

die and the ripe seeds develop into pendulous little purses – faerie poppets – covered with tiny hooks, which are caught on animals' fur or birds' plumage and may be carried many miles before they are finally shaken loose. The curious downward sweep of flower head and seed, contrasting with the upright buds makes this plant unusual and attractive (see Fig 38).

Like choirboys' collars, frilly bracts sit jauntily around the hazel nuts, but provide little protection against a determined dormouse (Plate 55). This is a 'full frontal' study, the attention of the subject is directed outwards, towards the viewer, unlike the profiles and semi-profiles of animals which we have attempted before. The nuts, too, are seen directly, and by careful use of radial stitching, a convex cone shape can be achieved which appears to be thrusting forwards. This is shown in Fig 40. For the uppermost nut, work a disc of *opus plumarium* within the jagged outer bract, leaving a voiding line to separate the two. At the apex of the nut, work a single seed stitch to seal the radial stitches and complete the motif. The nuts seen at an angle may be worked in the same way, by treating the apex as the central core for the radial work and, irrespective of the acuteness of the angle of stitching, working around the motif in a complete arc of 360 degrees. Remember

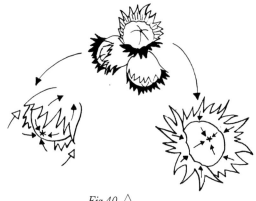

Fig 40 △
Hazel nuts. Open arrows indicate the
direction in which individual stitches should be
taken, while black arrows suggest the overall
sweep of the stitches towards the various core
growing points

PLATE 56 ▷

In the canopy of the oak tree two butterflies are equally at home – the purple hairstreak (left) and the purple emperor. The former relies almost entirely upon the oak for its survival and its Latin name bears witness to the close association: Quercusia quercus (quercus = oak). *Its dramatic upper colouring is shared by the purple emperor* (Apatura iris), *whose underside wing pattern is one of the most beautiful of all European butterflies. Remember the order in which wings should be worked (Fig. 5, page 19) and that the slightly more matt effect can be achieved by terminating the strata of radial stitching rather more abruptly than would be the case on the upper wing*
9 x 9cm (3½ x 3½ inches)

PLATE 57 ▷

The holly blue (Celastrina argiolus) *has been called the 'Christmas butterfly', not because it flies during the festive season, but because its caterpillars feed upon holly in the spring and ivy in the autumn. It cannot be confused with any other species of blue butterfly, as its delicate ice-blue underwing is unique. Work it as a single stratum of radial work and superimpose the black studding. The upper wing surfaces should be worked in a broad arc of blue, followed by very fine strata of white and black respectively*
9.0 x 10cm (3½ x 4 inches)

to make the bracts lighter on their uppermost surfaces, and to maintain the voiding lines throughout to separate the planes.

The same principle is applied to create the fuzzy, pear-shaped face and body of the dormouse. Initially, ignore features such as whiskers and work the little triangular nose, diamond-oval eyes and pert ears. Then, treating the nose as the core for your stitching, build up the radial work which will form the face. The strata will be sickle shaped as the dome of the head appears, and should be worked around the eyes and ears without breaking ranks. Leave a voiding line (which will be subdued later) between the head and the body and continue to build up the shape. With only these initial strata of stitching complete the effect will be stark (Fig 41, top). Now go on to soften the impression (bottom) by working fine straight stitching over the strata, and to subdue the voiding line, extending beyond the main body to create the soft, fluffy outer fur. Finally include the whiskers, black where they need to contrast the fur, white where they emerge against the black background. The tail is a single arc of softened river stitch (page 46).

Centrally veined leaves, such as the hazel with its rough ovate form and the rose leaf, toothed and serrated (shown with hips in Plate 55) while essentially similar in construction, can vary enormously in their overall shape. The smooth rounded lobes of the English oak, *Quercus robur* (Plate 56), could hardly form a

greater contrast with wickedly spiked holly in Plate 57. However, they both grow in similar locations, and might well be included in a single study. Careful shadow lining and the blending of several shades of green in a single leaf conveys the dull, matt quality of the oak. With a pale central vein, work in a 3/1F thread with three shades of green, gradually blending the colours together. The cups of the acorns on their long pipe-like stems are built up in closely worked dotting stitches, gradually darkening as they approach the shaded side of each motif.

The upper and lower surfaces of holly leaves are waxy, shiny above and slightly duller below. Their rigid, angular quality means that the spines appear to reflex sharply across the main body of the leaf and very careful attention must be paid to the opposite angle principle: the stitches on the underside of the leaf must be at exactly the same, but opposite, degree of radial working as those above. The spines are rarely green, more often a fleshy pink-brown, and should be worked in a single fine stitch at the same angle as the body of the leaf, if necessary directly superimposed upon the work underneath (see Fig 42).

Only female holly trees bear berries, although male and female have delightful little four-petalled flowers, the latter given a pinkish tinge by a red-tipped globular green pistil. A random scattering of these flowers amongst the leaves (Plate 57) is an effective device; worked simply, and without cluttering the design with individual stems and stalks, it gives lightness to a study.

Fig 41 △
The principles of radial stitching, individual strata and softening apply in whatever situation the subject may be found. This sleepy dormouse is sketched (top) as a series of oval shapes and the strata of stitches would be cut off abruptly between face and body, body and leg, etc, as it would in Plate 55. Below, the sweep of softening straight stitches is indicated by the finer lines following the contours of the body

HELEN
STEVENS

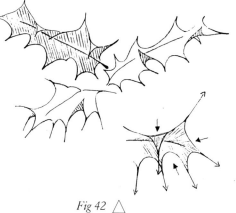

Fig 42 △
Holly leaves. In the topmost trio, the undersides of the leaves are hatched to indicate structure and the lowest of the three includes its sharp spines which should be overlaid after the rest of the leaf has been worked in the directions shown by the arrows (bottom)

. . . .

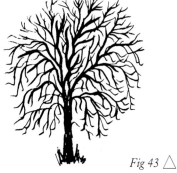

Fig 43 △

*Basically the same shape, the details of the
twigs and branches identify the winter
silhouettes of these three species: oak, beech and
ash. When 'dressed' with summer foliage they
will still be immediately identifiable*

PLATE 58 ▷

*'Fantasia'. However complicated or delicate
the details of an embroidery may eventually be,
the initial sketch should have some simplicity of
line which will act as a 'skeleton' upon which
to build. Here, the twin arches of the bramble
sweep unbroken from left to right: strong
elements which support the diverse filigree of
features around them. If you are right handed,
you will usually find it easier to work stem
stitch from right to left, and vice versa. If a
long arc must be worked in a direction which
you find uncomfortable, remember that you can
always turn the work upside down which will
temporarily reverse the direction*
Embroidery shown life size:
18 x 25.5cm (7 x 10 inches)

. . . .

FROST HOLLOW

As colours begin to deaden and leaves to fall with the onset of winter, plants, shrubs and trees take on a new personae. The protective screen of foliage which hid their secrets in the summer is gone and their structures are laid bare. Frost sparkles, twigs are etched sharply against a cold, bright sky and moonlight casts stark shadows on the frozen ground.

There is a brief transitional interlude between autumn and winter – before the last of the berries are taken and the first snow falls – with a special charm of its own (Plate 58). Country lore advises against eating blackberries *(Rubus fruticosus)* after Michaelmas (29 September), as the Devil spits on them on that night, but animals and birds hold no such superstition and in places the berries linger until November, providing a last feast for animals about to hibernate. The eggs of certain moths are laid within the leaves of the bramble and caterpillars burrow their way out, leaving veins exposed. As an alternative to honeycomb stitch, fine openly spaced radial stitching in the same colour as the central vein can convey these wounds, while a white and clear cellophane blending filament creates the sparkle of a frosted spider's web.

The bindweed which rioted up the blackberry stem in summer has paled to silver-grey, its leaves mushroom-brown and drooping. Using a silver metallic thread, couch a single strand in twists and coils for the upper tendrils and further down, where the leaves meet the main stem bring the leaf stalks smoothly down to join it, finally allowing several couched threads to lie side by side to create a solid structure.

Take a walk at this time of the year and pay particular attention to colours. Any preconceived ideas that late autumn is a time only of gold and brown will soon vanish. Extraordinary combinations of crimson and pale creamy greens combine with mulberry shot, earthy duns and caramels. The strange, ethereal winter moth *(Operophtera brumata)* is a common sight as it seeks out the sweetness of late fruit – combine these natural elements with the fantasy of falling snowflakes or tiny cruciform stars in a winter sky.

When winter arrives in earnest, the majesty of great unclothed trees is finally apparent. Their massive trunks often submerged in a mass of clambering ivy, an occasional bough still retaining a scant dusting of brown leaves, they loom above a hard-bitten landscape. In Plate 59 the noble English oak points the way home. Try sketching the silhouettes of winter trees (see Fig 43) and you will soon become aware of how different they are: the oak with its stocky, sturdy trunk and large branches which rise to form a massive crown, the beech with its spreading, horizontal profile, the ash's tall straight trunk and delicately uplifted outer twigs.

When a final sketch has been prepared, transfer it carefully on to your background fabric – until you become confident that you can work the correctly shaped twigs freehand, do not skimp in transferring *all* the detail. Begin by working the trunk, dashing in the upright stitches boldly from the base of the tree

upwards. The lower boughs are not sinuous, flexible structures like the pliant stems of smaller plants, but a strong, rigid framework which supports the rest of the tree. The dashing should branch off from below. When the main branches have been worked, the smaller branches and twigs can be added, in straight stitching, narrowing the gauge of thread toward the outer edges.

If the tree is to be clothed in summer leaves (Plates 32, 39, 40, etc) it is now ready. Pay some attention to the arrangement of leaves on individual twigs, and to their overall shape, but remember that at this distance it is first impressions that count. Work leaves on the upper side of twigs in a lighter shade than those below, and do not be tempted to fill in gaps between branches with random leafing – trees are not solid structures: the light between the branches is as important as the branches themselves.

In Plate 59, the coppery beech hedge is echoed by the copper-red leaves which still hang in patches on the oak. Elsewhere on the tree random 'birds' nests' of mistletoe cluster, worked as very fine, unstructured masses of stem stitch,

PLATE 59 ▽

'The Road Home'. With very little other colour in this study, an indication of a distant frost-bright blue sky leads the eye on into the far distance. At the horizon it is hardly a shade darker than the snow, deepening almost imperceptibly as it zigzags away to nothingness. Above, a sketchy suggestion of circling birds adds movement

16 x 10cm (6¼ x 4 inches)

dotted with white seed stitching (the berries). The snow lies featureless, save for a darker area indicating the path, and beyond the stile the village lies nestling in the distance, only its rooftops visible as minute trails of smoke (tiny dot stitches) rise into the air.

Working on black, exactly the same techniques are used to create the needle-lace effect of tree against sky (Plate 60). The moon, a couched circle and sickle, the latter infilled with silver silk, casts shadows to the left, and the trunks are appropriately darker to that side. In the moonlight the long-dead purple flowers of the heather still retain a brownish-mauve, rough texture, created by dotting in the shadowed areas in contrast to the smoothly worked straight stitching elsewhere. The lime-loving common ash *(Fraxinus excelsior)* is at home on the bleak winter moors, its grey-green twigs tipped with silver already concealing the buds of the coming spring.

PLATE 60 △
The wind was a torrent of darkness
among the gusty trees,
The moon was a ghostly galleon
tossed upon cloudy seas,
The road was a ribbon of moonlight
over the purple moor · · ·

The Highwayman
Alfred Noyes
15.5 x 13cm (6 x 5 inches)

· · · · · · · ·

◁ PLATE 61
*The glorious plumage of the peacock on the cool,
sculpted lawns of a fine country house. Both the
cedar tree* (Cedrus libani) *and the Japanese
maple* (Acer palmatum) *were favourite
parkland trees during the eighteenth and
nineteenth centuries; their distinctive,
spreading boughs must be embroidered before
their clothing of leaves. Yew* (Taxus baccata)*,
here flanking the informal drive, may be
clipped into a variety of shapes which are
equally satisfying in their embroidered form*
Embroidery shown life size:
33 x 21.5cm (13 x 8½ inches)

CHAPTER SIX

GILDING THE LILY

*With enchanting murmurs, Daisy admired
this aspect or that of the feudal silhouette
against the sky, admired the gardens, the
sparkling odour of jonquils and the frothy
odour of hawthorn and plum blossoms and the
pale gold odour of kiss-me-at-the-gate.*

The Great Gatsby
F. Scott Fitzgerald

PEACOCKS AND PARADISE

Stately, sweeping lawns, grand houses, landscaped parkland, sculpted lakes, follies, gazebos and arbours – nature perfected and tamed, brought to heel by the hand of man. How different from the tumbling, massed exuberance of the cottage garden – but in its way equally typical of another facet of the countryside today.

If the cottage garden incorporated and built upon wild flowers and shrubs to create its own particular identity, the stately home and its grounds has exerted its influence on the countryside in reverse. Architecture, landscape design, trees, shrubs, animals and birds native to far flung corners of the world have been gathered together during successive generations of inventive building, grand tours and passionate collecting. Originally restricted to their new, enclosed habitats, such flora and fauna as could adapt, soon outstripped their captive environment to become familiar, and occasionally unwelcome, features of the wild. For the country embroiderer they provide fresh impetus and inspiration.

There can be no creature which has been more extensively used as a source of design and decoration than the peacock – the male Indian peafowl *(Pavo cristatus)*. His wiry crest, shimmering plumage and iridescent, glittering train have been interpreted for millennia in innumerable cultures from the Pharaohs of Egypt to the William Morris Arts and Crafts movement and beyond; but amid these many stylized creations a truly lifelike study is rarely attempted – which is a pity because beyond the geometric precision of arc and angle, colour and poise, there is a real flesh-and-blood bird trying to get out! Embroidery is an ideal medium in which to capture that reality (see Plate 61).

Essentially, the body of the peacock can be worked in exactly the same manner as the body of any other bird. Choose the gauge of your thread bearing in mind the scale to which you will be working, and remember that this must be maintained throughout. The peacock is a large bird which you will probably be reducing considerably, so a single fine thread may well serve to interpret a substantial feather filament (see detail in Plate 62).

The peacock is a type of pheasant (actually a big chicken, related to the red junglefowl, ancestor of all domestic fowl) and his fluffy 'drawers' are, indeed, reminiscent of the farmyard hen. They are black, with reddish undertones and entirely overshadowed by his showy upper parts. The first features of his plumage which present a new challenge are the fan-shaped feathers of his lower back, which, as he raises his tail, also begin to arch upwards. From this point we must begin to treat each feather separately. These base feathers should be worked as small arcs of radial stitching.

It is, of course, the tail which is the greatest feature and the greatest test. Basically there are two types of tail feather – the majority include the familiar 'eye', while the others form an outer band of the longest feathers tipped with an inverted arrow (see Fig 44). Work the 'eyes' first, either in a three-strata Dalmatian-dog *opus plumarium* or, if your scale is very small, in ticking and/or

Fig 44 △

Peacock feathers. While the long, loose filaments may be suggested by floating embroidery (see page 41, Fig 15), the eye markings and sickles should be built up in radial stitching, the strata blending together where indicated by the hatched lines

studding. With reference to Fig 44 for structure, take a long straight stitch from the eye down to the rump of the bird, breaking it only if necessary to disappear behind another eye. Loosely work the shaft filaments of the feathers in a short floating stitch to create the effect of softness and movement, allowing them to become looser and longer towards the base of the tail. Finally, work the outer tail feathers in an arc around the main fan of the tail. The top-knot of green feathers forming the head crest may now be superimposed.

The magnificent display of the peacock in his breeding plumage is, of course, designed to impress his mate, though as a secondary function it intimidates rivals. The peacock butterfly has evolved a similar wing pattern solely to ward off predators, its four false 'eyes' designed to startle attacking birds (Plate 63). Of all the common European butterflies, it has the largest deterrent 'eyes' and its unique, prominently veined wing structure means that in embroidery it must be treated rather differently. Most wing patterns call for *opus plumarium* with varying amounts of Dalmatian-dog technique worked radially towards the body of the insect (see the red admiral in Plate 10). However, the four veins on the upper wing of the peacock mean that the six fields of red must be worked independently, leaving a fine voiding line, which must then be filled in with a 'tramline' of narrow stem stitch (see Fig 45). Fortunately, the peacock is one of

PLATE 62 △

Detail of Plate 61. Remember that the use of perspective can play some strange tricks on your choice of threads. The peacock is a large bird, but compared to a stately home it is tiny. However, with the bird in the foreground the roles are reversed. The filaments of the peacock's tail (bottom left) are worked in a single very fine strand of silk, stitched straight for the rigid elements of the feathers and left 'floating' elsewhere. The same gauge of thread is used on the frames of the central windows on the house, with only slightly thicker threads used to block in the rest of the building. The distance between the two principal elements serves to 'even out' the difference which would otherwise necessitate the use of a much thicker thread for the house

Dimensions of detail shown:
17 x 10.5cm (6½ x 4 inches)

PLATE 63 △

The peacock butterfly (Inachis io) *and the rhododendron. Two uses of fine overlaying stitch are shown in this study: first, the stamens bursting out of the flowers, in fine green silk laid directly over whatever feature may be beneath, and second the narrow 'railway tracks' on the top of the forewing of the butterfly (see also Fig 45). Whenever you overlay fine strands in this way try to ensure that the underlying embroidery is at a different angle from that which you are working. Even a slight variance will do — but if the angle is too similar the topmost stitches will simply merge into the base work*

15 x 16.5cm (5¾ x 6½ inches)

the most common butterflies and may easily be examined at close quarters. To attract them to your garden simply leave a patch of nettles growing wild – they will bask obligingly with their upper wings extended over their lower. The more smoothly you merge your fields of colour in the spectacular 'eyes' the better you will capture that glossy, jewelled surface.

The rhododendron was first introduced into Britain in 1763 from Armenia (then Pontus, in Asia Minor), initially as an attractive parkland shrub, then, when its tenacious propensity to establish itself in the wild was fully appreciated, as cover for game. Unfortunately for the native flora it then spread like wildfire, able to colonize not only heathland (where it shaded out less robust plants), but thriving even beneath dense woodland growth and exhausting the soil. It is tolerant of most weed-killers and cannot be destroyed by harsh cutting back. In short, it is now regarded by many as a pest, but it is nevertheless a beautiful shrub with complex candlesticks of flowers bursting out of whorled clusters of handsome, waxy leaves.

It is an evergreen shrub, flowering in May and June, when it produces bunches of blossom – up to 15 blooms on a single head framed by a saucer-like arrangement of leaves. As a subject for embroidery it must be approached cautiously, the design built up with forethought, rather than cursed in hindsight! A dozen blooms all jostling for position might be delightful in real life, but as an embroidered study would be a jumbled mass of small areas of apparently disjointed fields of stitching – no whole flower would be identifiable. It is much better to choose a head with fewer blooms – preferably in various stages of opening – each of which can be treated individually. Now we have an uninterrupted view of at least some flowers to act as necessary reference points when others are partly hidden from view (see also Fig 46). Treat each petal (or part petal) separately with stitches running towards the centre of the bloom. The huge variety of hybrid rhododendrons means that the colour choice is entirely yours, although with the use of a shadow line to define individual petals a paler rather than darker shade is probably the more effective. If the study were worked on a black background, with the more prominent effect of voiding, a deeper colour could be striking, as in the case of the hibiscus in Plate 64.

The fact that certain plants and creatures might not be suited to a temperate climate did not prevent their being brought to grace the homes of the rich. Ingenuity invariably came to the rescue, orchid houses, aviaries and conservatories were heated and humidified to accommodate them. During the eighteenth century, the exploration of the New World resulted in the importation of exotic flowers, butterflies and bird species of incredible diversity. Captain Cook's charting of the Pacific Islands began a vogue for all things tropical – the hibiscus began to run riot in the Old World.

The decorative properties of this beautiful flower are immediately apparent, but not always easy to convey. The large, fleshy petals disappear into a deep, shadowed throat, and must be worked in at least three strata of radial stitching,

Fig 45 △

The 'railway lines' along the top of the upper wings of the peacock butterfly are laid over the existing embroidery (1) while the 'tramlines' forming the veins of the wing should be created by a fine line of voiding which may then be filled with a narrow stem stitch if desired (2)

Fig 46 △

The pink hybrid rhododendron 'Tessa', is one of the simpler forms of this shrub

the upper petals apparently terminating abruptly where they curve away to the throat (Fig 47). The prominent yellow stamens and gold-red stigma may be enhanced with a few touches of metallic thread, while the striking yellow-green foliage is worked simply, the centrally veined leaves ovate and lightly serrated.

Still more exotic is the aptly named marvellous spatule-tail hummingbird *(Loddigesia mirabilis)* from the high Andes in Peru. Its body barely 12.5cm (5 inches long), is only one-third the length of its fabulous tail, made up of only four feathers, two of them peacock-like. During courtship the male frames his iridescent throat feathers with these 'eye-feathers' and flies back and forth in front of his prospective mate. Here is an opportunity, once again, to use a subtle blending filament to achieve this iridescent effect. The bottle-green back of the bird and its vibrant blue head can both benefit from the added sparkle of a separated filament which should be incorporated in your own specially constructed 2/1F or 3/1F thread. The lyre shape formed by the interlacing of the tail feathers, is purposely asymmetrical to create perspective – but pay particular attention to the directional working of the stem stitch on the outer feathers (in both cases the outer edges of each stitch facing downwards) and soften the outline of the inner feathers by overlaying fine strands of silk.

Orchids have been cultivated since antiquity for their beauty and supposedly aphrodisiac properties. The latter is unproven, but the extraordinary shapes and colours of the many genera and species (the family is the second largest in the botanical kingdom) is beyond question. Hothouse varieties now come from all parts of the world, two of the most popular genera are the Coelogynes and the Cymbidiums (Plate 65).

Worked on black, nothing is more spectacular than the striped, barred and spotted petals of the orchid flower, contrasted with the clean, straight lines of its strong and vigorous leaves. Cymbidiums (the larger flowers in Plate 65) originate from Asia and Australia and vary in colour through white, cream, yellow, pink,

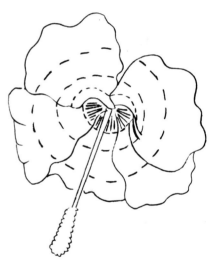

◁ *PLATE 64*

The hibiscus shown here is Hibiscus rosa-sinensis *or Chinese shoeflower. All over the tropics they are used for personal decoration, particularly in Hawaii where they are fashioned into the famous 'leis' used to greet visitors. As in Plate 58, two primary sweeps form the framework for this study, which are then dressed with the more complicated elements of the design. The tendrils of gold thread are purely a decorative device to add interest to an otherwise dull corner – they were couched freehand and allowed to develop spontaneously*
16.5 x 26cm (6½ x 10¼ inches)

Fig 47 ▷

(Top) The basic outline of the hibiscus appears flat and without form.
(Centre) The innermost strata should be worked in a very dark shade – even black – and surrounded by at least three strata of radial opus plumarium, *as shown by the hatched line.*
(Bottom) A three-dimensional effect quickly builds up

PLATE 65 ▷
Cymbidium *'Queen of Gatton'* and
Coelogyne nitida *are relatively easy to grow*
in temperate climates, given the protection of a
greenhouse or conservatory. If you are fortunate
enough to be able to study orchids first hand you
will be dazzled by the choice of subject matter
for the embroiderer. Try to resist the temptation
to cram too much colour and outlandish form
into a single study. Here, while the shapes are
extraordinary, the colours are fairly muted.
In Plate 64 the colours are vibrant and exotic,
but the contours of the design restrained.
A successful study should intrigue rather
than startle!
10.5 x 17.5cm (4 x 6¾ inches)

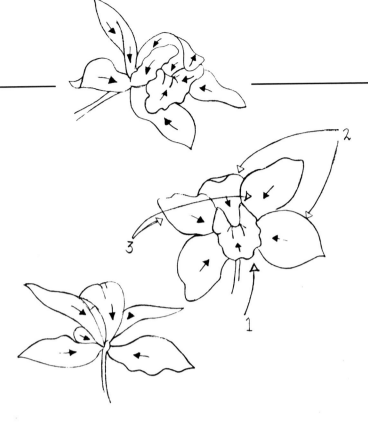

◁ Fig 48
The cymbidium orchid from three angles.
(1) the lower lip, (2) sepals, (3) petals. The
black arrows indicate the directional
flow of the stiches

red, green and brown, usually with bold lip markings in other shades. It is useful to have some understanding of the anatomy of a complicated flower such as this (see Fig 48) in order to know in which direction the segments of radial stitching should flow. Once this is established, the various fields of the petals should be worked accordingly, the lip and throat markings incorporated through Dalmatian-dog technique, and the stripes superimposed by means of shooting stitch. Similarly the more delicate Coelogynes should be worked with reference to their natural structure and pendulous habit. The leaves are a real test of skill in *opus plumarium* and snake stitch. Single stitches may be up to 6cm (2¼ inches) long, so make sure that your fabric is mounted correctly in your frame and is taut enough to support them.

SMALL IS BEAUTIFUL

So far when we have looked at miniaturization it has been as part of a larger study – the bird, plant or animal has been a means to an end – placing various features into perspective. The same process must be approached slightly differently if we are to create a miniature in its own right. For centuries true miniatures have been collected and admired – there is always a certain fascination in discovering just how much detail can be incorporated into a very tiny study. Many stately homes have entire rooms set aside to display such collections. What are the special considerations which must be brought to bear in an embroidered miniature?

First, the picture itself must be a complete entity. Everything must be to scale. Plates 66, 67 and 68 are all reproduced life size. Each has been designed to fill its respective frame effectively. In Plate 66 an entire landscape has been included, stretching away to the distant horizon. By contrast, Plate 67 is more

PLATE 66 ▷
*Every little girl's dream: a pure white pony,
mane and tail blowing in the wind and open
fields in which to ride him. Even in a tiny
study such as this it is possible to create
atmosphere as well as action. Helped by the
curve of the frame, the tree is tossed to the
right, and the breeze takes the pony's coat in the
same direction. By varying the shades of green
in the fields beyond, an impression of sunshine
alternating with passing clouds is given, which
is echoed by the use of matt and floss silk for the
minute trees on the horizon*
10.25 x 10.25cm (4 x 4 inches)
including frame

PLATE 67 ▷
*'The Fox Cub'. The choice of an oval frame for
this miniature was to emphasize the close,
intimate nature of the subject matter. The
young, snub-nosed cub has not yet achieved the
sleek lines of its elders, it stays hidden, merging
itself as far as possible with its surroundings.
Miniature work invites the closest inspection.
Make sure that there are no loose 'tails' of
thread on the reverse of your embroidery – they
will be seen through the fabric and ruin your
outline*
6.5 x 8.5cm (2½ x 3¼ inches)
including frame

◁ *PLATE 68*

The broad wing-span of the kestrel means that at its widest it will fill the field of the circular frame, while leaving other areas bare. This does not matter as (even in miniature) it is important to allow a feeling of 'space' above and beyond a bird in flight. Roughly centralize the body of the bird and a natural perspective will develop – open above and allowing the positioning of the tiny landscape below to balance the area filled by the tail. Notes on the mounting and framing of circular, oval and miniature embroideries are included in Appendix B
10.25 x 10.25cm (4 x 4 inches) including frame

Fig 49 △
Design for a miniature. A green woodpecker above a tiny tree. The tree is shown as it would be transferred – without leafing – but the embroidery would include foliage

intimate: the fox cub remains in its covert, grasses and wildflowers grow up around and between its paws, the curve of its back echoed by the dense-leaved bush. In Plate 68 there is even a miniature within a miniature. The kestrel hovers above a minute landscape, the ploughed field warm in the evening sunlight. The basic techniques which create these frameworks are identical to those in full-sized studies – the straight and seed stitching for trees, horizontal stitching for the grassy uplands and impressionistic interpretation for the flowers. For the main subject of each, however, new guidelines come into play.

In Plates 41 and 43 we discussed how to extrapolate only the essential features of a subject and work them to complement the greater detail elsewhere in the study. In a true miniature as many tiny details as possible must be included – but on a much reduced scale. The first prerequisite is fine thread. It is impossible to work extremely fine details in a heavy thread. If possible use silk (split floss down to the narrowest gauge you can manage). If this is not possible, experiment with cottons, splitting down threads into their component strands. You may need to expand your palette of colours as you will not be able to create graduations of shade through mixing strands in 3/1 or 4/1 threads.

Break yourself in gently by attempting subjects which do not include too many intricate markings. The white pony in Plate 66 is worked in three shades – white, light grey and dark grey – with, of course, the essential shadow line. Both here and in Plate 67 the directional play of light upon the stitches is important to create roundness and movement. The fox cub's fur is worked in two shades of

Fig 50 △
'The Embroiderer's Arms'

red-brown. It merges into the white and black of its chest and brush distinctly, but on the foreleg shooting stitch has been used to soften the change of colour (on a full-sized study, several strata of darkening shades would be used here). Do not overlook tiny, but fundamental, touches such as the highlight in each animal's eye.

Once used to working on this reduced scale you will soon feel confident to attempt an even more demanding subject. The banding and barring on the female kestrel is obviously too small to be included when your design is initially transferred on to fabric, so keep a handbook close by for later reference. Shadow line the head, body, leg coverts and each of the tail, primary and secondary feathers. Work the face, legs, body and tail graduating your colours according to your palette, and the wing structure in the usual order (primaries, secondaries, wing coverts and finally the lower part of the underwing, where it meets the body). You will now have a creamy brown, but unmarked bird. Short shooting stitches in radiating bands will form the barring on the wing and tail feathers, while the markings on the head, breast and underwing areas can be created by the use of delicate ticking stitches. Try to keep them uniform and in rank. The tiny landscape below is shown sweeping forwards, the ploughed furrows fanning out towards the foreground. The merest suggestion of sky is all that is needed to bring the elements of the study together.

There need be no restriction on your imagination when it comes to creating successful miniatures. Butterflies and flowers make a delightful combination (Plate 4, page 8), a tiny church or cottage, a summerhouse set amid garden flower beds, even a favourite holiday location (Fig 50). The world in microcosm is at your fingertips.

THE HUNTER AND THE HUNTED

The broad acres of landscaped parkland and managed woods which are an integral part of many country estates are not only beautiful but also vital protected habitats for many truly wild creatures. The gamekeeper who sees that deer and pheasant remain unmolested by poachers is also, perhaps unwittingly, ensuring the privacy of badgers and woodcock. But life in the animal kingdom, even without the intervention of man, is often a question of kill or be killed and no objective collection of pictures would be complete without including nature's harsher aspect.

How beautiful and yet how ruthless is the ambush of the sparrowhawk. Its relatively short wings allow it manoeuvrability in quite dense woodland cover and its favourite method of hunting is to wait motionless on a stump or fencepost until an unsuspecting small bird is within range. A flurry of wings, a scattering of feathers, and usually it is all over, although there are occasions when the prey may be just a little too agile (Plate 69).

With no foliage to distract the eye, no landscape to soften the contours, this study is as dramatic in format as it is in content. All the attention is focused upon

PLATE 69 ▷
Dr Dolittle's cheeky cockney sparrow, Cheapside, typifies the image of the cocky little bird always able to achieve one final great escape. The sparrowhawk (Accipiter nisus) rarely misses less street-wise prey: in winter it can be seen circling high above unwary finches and buntings feeding together in great unprotected flocks. Try to give your subjects characters of their own – a flying feather, highlighted eye or strategically pointed needle-sharp claw can speak volumes
22.5 x 28cm (8¾ x 11 inches)

HELEN
STEVENS

the action and the actors. In the miniature study of the kestrel (Plate 68) we abandoned the Dalmatian-dog technique in favour of ticking and shooting stitches because of the tiny scale; here we can return to more expressive methods. The smooth, exquisitely marked plumage of the sparrowhawk must, of course, be worked in a single plane. All the principal markings, the chevrons on chest and legs, and the barring on primary and secondary feathers should be embroidered first before the creamy gold body colour and whitish wing and tail feathers are built up around them. Remember to work each primary feather separately, taking a long central stitch down from its tip towards the body (the main vein), incorporating the filaments of the feathers in symmetrically opposed angles on either side. Revert to ticking for the finest markings such as on the throat and underwing areas.

The eye and beak structure on birds of prey is distinctive (see Fig 51). Unlike many smaller birds they have a coloured iris which adds to the apparent menace of their stare, an inner eye ring and prominent 'cere' capping the beak above the nostril. Try to familiarize yourself with these features in sketch form before attempting to embroider them. They will require fine thread and close attention to outlining and directional stitching.

The house sparrow *(Passer domesticus)*, while having the dubious honour of lending its name to the sparrowhawk, is by no means its most common prey; other small woodland birds probably make up more than 75 per cent of its diet. Ever since man first began to build houses, the house sparrow has largely abandoned its original woodland habitat and relied upon humans, at least partly, for food and shelter. It is so common that it is often ignored as a design subject – and yet it is actually quite a pretty bird, especially the male, with its chocolate-brown, barred wings and tail, silver-grey underparts and distinctive black bib.

If sparrows have made their homes under your eaves you will find no shortage of small, soft, downy feathers to examine as they fall from nests during fledging and feeding. These are entirely different from the tough, protective flight feathers of the upper body, and in embroidery should be treated delicately, allowed to swirl and flutter unshadowed in varying shades. Using a fine thread, work a central vein in stem stitch, curving it slightly. Run angled stitches off this core, to either side, allowing the quill a short tail at the end. Embroider the falling feathers randomly – they should appear as spontaneous and lively as the escape itself. This, after all, is the one that got away!

◁ *Fig 51*
The beautiful head of the buzzard shows
the distinctive 'cere' which caps the wicked
beak and the striking eye (dark pupilled with
an orange iris) which can be highlighted to
great effect. Pencil lines show the direction
of the stitches

CHAPTER SEVEN

LAND'S END

*I am reminded of a certain Sunday morning
on the beach, the bells ringing for church . . .
and the sun away at sea, just breaking through
the heavy mist, and showing us the ships,
like their own shadows.*

David Copperfield
Charles Dickens

HELEN
STEVENS

FLOTSAM AND JETSAM

Perpetual motion. Even at its most calm the sea is never entirely still. The tide edges forward and is pulled back, pebbles become wet, and dry, changing colour before your eyes, seaweed swirls and seabirds circle overhead.

Explore the water in Plate 70. By now, it is unnecessary to enumerate each technique – you will readily identify which has been used where. The sea is rolling in. Wavelets splash on to rocks. The surf is low, but regular, with areas of relative calm between each surge. Observation has been the key to putting this study together – and a simplified sketch of the water helped in deciding where dotting should give way to straight stitching and vice versa (see Fig 52). Surges and splashes have been superimposed over rocks in places, and the stones themselves appear partly buried in the sand.

A suggestion of unexpected colour in the sky echoes the sandy seashore, its texture light and airy contrasting the grainy, stranded cotton effect of the sand, and the tern in flight is pale, icy grey-blue as it wings over its mate.

The foreground and framing elements of the picture are again worked in techniques which need no further explanation. They are by now familiar, but here must be used to their most subtle effect – the breast of the roseate tern reveals a delicate rosy flush which must blend imperceptibly into its snowy white plumage and the large, paper-thin petals of the sea bindweed and the evening primrose show no sharply delineated strata, but rather smooth, open-faced sweeps of even stitching.

Seashore plants have a tendency to appear alien – perhaps it is simply against our expectations to see vigorous growth springing from apparently inhospitable sand – but their strange ethereal beauty, combined with other features of the water's edge can produce some lovely results in embroidery. Plate 72 shows sea holly *(Eryngium maritmum)*, its thistly leaves and metallic blue, globe-like flowers once a common sight on beaches and sand dunes. The leaves are worked like their namesakes (ordinary holly) shown in Plate 57, aqua blue-green, paler beneath and with wicked spines, added once the body of each leaf has been completed. The flower heads, however, are complicated and must be worked in several stages. First, outline each individual floret in fine black thread. Then, in blue, work the tiny petals, which appear heart-shaped. Above each floret dot in two or three yellow-tipped stamens and finally work the small spiny bracts (which give the head its prickly appearance) in chevron stitch. This order of working is set out in Fig. 53.

What visit to the seaside is complete without beachcombing for shells? There are an enormous variety to be found around the coasts of Britain alone – farther-flung places provide still greater scope – and all those shown in Plate 72 are fairly widespread. Possibly the most common is the edible cockle (centre), and certainly one of the easiest to embroider. Begin by outlining each ridge and then, using a 3/1F thread which can be gradually lightened by increasing the ratio of

◁ *PLATE 70*

The cool blue-green breath of the sea seems to envelope the shore until even the plants appear languid. Bindweed flourishes on sand dunes and the delicate yellow petals of the evening primrose (Oenothera rubricaulis)*, closed during the day, are so keen to welcome the evening that they can be seen to open with the naked eye, their pervasive perfume calming and soporific. Thrift* (Armeria maritima *ssp.* maritima) *nestles low amongst the seashore pebbles, its tiny flower heads worked in seed stitches. The roseate tern* (Sterna dougallii) *lives up to its 'rosy' name only during the breeding season when an ethereal pink flush suffuses its breast. Its nest is the merest scrape in amid the stones above the high watermark. Each stone is treated separately in embroidery, outlined to one side and infilled with straight stitching. Larger rocks along the tide line are worked in perpendicular straight stitching, the horizontal stitches representing water and sand overlapping their base*

Embroidery shown life size:
20.5 x 25.5cm (8 x 10 inches)

◁ *PLATE 71*
*Detail of Plate 70. Where the pink glow of the
evening sky is reflected in the water, single
strands of fine floss silk are interspersed amid
the 2/1T threads used to create the broad
expanse of sea. Untwisted silk is also used on
the breakers. The white sails of the yachts are
well defined against the sunset, their reflections
merging into the distant grey-green sea*
Dimensions of detail shown:
12.5 x 15.5cm (5 x 6 inches)

Fig 52 ▷
*The tide lapping in. Without the distraction of
other elements the movement of the water can
be simplified down to a few lines. The 'white
horses' are then worked in white and ice-blue
dotting, the risers of each wave in dark
straight stitching, and the rest of the water in
varying shades*

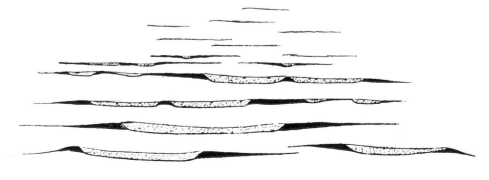

pale thread to dark towards the top of the shell, work your way up through the ridges from the bottom, infilling each with a single arc of snake stitch, allowing the stitches to merge toward the 'nose' of the shell.

The cockle has a double shell; single-shelled molluscs are more difficult to approach. Apart from limpets, they are generally spiralled – and often delightfully patterned. Far left in Plate 72 is the large necklace shell, very like a common snail. It can be worked simply as a spiral of satin stitch, having first shadow lined the lower edges of the coils, its markings incorporated as work progresses. The netted dog whelk (far right) should be outlined, each coil infilled with reddish brown, and then 'laddered' with white to create a pattern of small squares.

The tower shell (second right) looks like a small, delicately coloured unicorn horn with a rough, uneven surface. Again, outline each coil separately and then build up the ridges of the spiral by working irregularly spaced stem stitch in decreasing ranks from the base of the shell towards its tip.

Finally, we come to the common starfish, the prize exhibit in any small child's bucket! The dull spines on the top of the animal's skin make it appear warty in texture and so, like the toad in Plate 28 (page 45), it is built up in dotting stitch, with variations in colour giving it contour. The common starfish ranges in colour from yellowish orange to red and purple, though it is always paler towards the centre and the 'star' effect can be emphasized by white dotting overlaid at the ridge of each leg and at its core.

Humans are not the only beachcombers to enjoy the seashore. *Rattus rattus*, the ship rat, while often the victim of a bad press, is actually a clean and timid animal left to its own devices, only seeking refuge in barns and warehouses when cold weather necessitates. On protected islands, such as Lundy, off the north coast

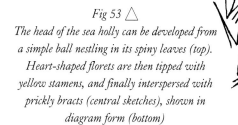

Fig 53 △
The head of the sea holly can be developed from a simple ball nestling in its spiny leaves (top). Heart-shaped florets are then tipped with yellow stamens, and finally interspersed with prickly bracts (central sketches), shown in diagram form (bottom)

◁ *PLATE 72*
The Queen of Spain fritillary (Argynnis lathonia) *is a rare European migrant to Britain, most likely to be found close to southern coasts. The white 'quick-silver' markings on the lower wings actually reflect the light like tiny mirrors, and a very slim metallic silver thread has been used as one strand in a 3/1F thread to catch and shimmer certain lights. From left to right the shells (common names in the main text) are:* Natica catena, Asterias rubens, Cerastoderma edule, Turritella communis *and* Nassarius reticulatus
13 x 17cm (5 x 6½ inches)

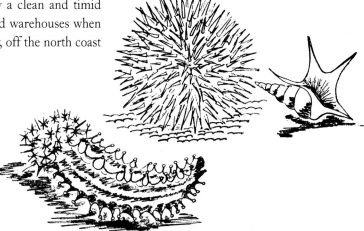

Fig 54 △
There is no shortage of strange shapes on the seashore – the sea urchin (centre), pelican's foot shell (right), and sea cucumber (left)

of Devon, open-air colonies feed exclusively on plant matter, but, ever the opportunist, a rat will take advantage of whatever may be on offer and along populated coasts will raid ships' stores and docks just as it did centuries ago.

An agile climber (Plate 73) the rat makes an unusual study – an elaboration of the idea behind Plate 19 (page 33). The narrow rope has been worked in rows of stem stitch, closely packed, to give a fibrous texture, and the idea of the long tapered tail (the rat uses it for balance) interlacing rope and climbing plant appealed to me. The rat is a vagabond, a wayfarer, in this picture and to pursue this theme of escapism I chose to include the dewberry (a lesser-known relative of the common blackberry) as his prize. The fruits of the dewberry are clouded by a bloom of silver grey, each made up of several small berries clustered bramble-like on long runners. I have suggested this bloom by incorporating a strand of silver-mauve in a 3/1F thread, which appears as random streaks in the berries themselves. The strong trefoil leaves are bright green, again given a hint of bluish bloom by strands of aqua.

Scrambling past the last of the berries, on an Indian rope trick to who knows where, *Rattus* takes us beyond the tide-line which marks the boundary of the countryside we recognize. But, as the Mock Turtle sang to Alice,

What matters it how far we go . . .
There is another shore you know,
Upon the other side.

Alice in Wonderland
Lewis Carroll

THE GLOBAL VILLAGE

Journeys which once took days are now completed in hours. The other side of the world is now a day's flight away, and plants, birds and animals which were once only distant rumours to be wondered at in bestiaries and herbals are the stuff of television documentaries, telescopic photography and scientific research. We are the first generation of embroiderers literally to have the sky as our limit. Subjects which we cannot study at first hand in wildlife parks or botanical gardens we can examine in books and on video. Why restrict ourselves, therefore, to the countryside of one nation?

From the mountains of the Old World, to the forests of the New, inspiration is waiting. The tropics may have been 'imported' into the stately homes of Europe, but what could be more exotic than the bejewelled caps of the *Soldanella* literally breaking through the ice of a spring morning high in the Alps (Plate 74). No more than 5cm (2 inches or so) tall, their deeply serrated, bell-shaped flowers sparkle with melted snow – here a blending filament has been incorporated in the thread to imitate the effect. Velvet-green leaves sweep in an arc towards the base of

PLATE 73 ▷

When framed, a window mount would be cut to fit this study allowing the rope top right and bottom left to disappear from the field of vision. Don't be afraid to experiment with new ideas for mounting pictures. Double mounts – one window on top of another, allowing a border of about 3 or 4mm (⅛–¼ inch) – are useful to draw the eye into a study, and colours should be chosen to complement the subject matter
19 x 22cm (7½ x 8½ inches)

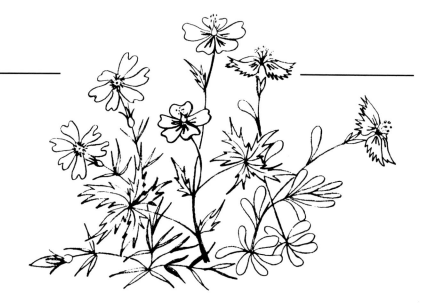

Fig 55 ▷
Many common garden plants have their
counterparts as Alpines. The Alpine geranium,
phlox and pink would make a delightful,
simple embroidery

the plant (an extreme example of radiating *opus plumarium*) and the first wisps of spring grass thrust through the snow – horizontal and vertical straight stitching.

In the New World, it was once said by immigrants that everything was bigger than it was at home! Certainly the inspiration is boundless. Plate 75 is a celebration of the links between Britain and Canada. Much of the subject matter was unfamiliar to me – the ground-cover plant *trillium*, so called because of its many tripartite characteristics (three sepals, three petals, three-whorled leaves) and the colourful, jaunty blue jay *(Cyanocitta cristata)*. Working studies of flora and fauna with which we are not well acquainted presents certain challenges. As we have discussed, it is the unique characteristics of a bird and its way of moving

PLATE 74 ▷
It might be tempting to include a small butterfly
or other insect in a study such as this – but
make sure you do your research first! The
Soldanella alpina *appears on its native hills*
before butterflies are in flight. The plants
actually melt the snow around them by
generating heat as they grow, forming a
delightful picture against a snowy background.
Fine, clear blending filaments have been
included throughout the embroidery (not just on
the flowers) to enhance this frosty subject
10 x 9cm (4 x 3½ inches)

which give it individuality and expression. If we have only seen a bird on paper it can be difficult to achieve a lively reality. Try to obtain as many pictures as possible, both photographs and sketches, taken from a variety of angles; profile, frontal, and especially showing the bird in action. Those dull; 'bird on a perch' shots in many bird-watchers' handbooks may be fine for identification purposes, but they say nothing of character. Pin your collection around the room and become familiar with your subject from all sides. Only then put together a composite study of the bird.

Similarly, plants which we cannot see and touch may seem unfamiliar and clumsy to embroider. We know how a pansy or a poppy *feels* – but is a *trillium* fleshy or floppy, are the leaves waxy or soft to the touch? A good handbook, as well as giving illustrations of the flower in question, should also describe its habit of growth and the texture of its foliage. Read the text, as well as looking at the pictures! You will then know whether to choose silk or cotton, fine one-stranded floss thread or a 4/1 T.

Imagery, too, can be fun. Great Anglo-Saxon embroideries often had a tale to tell and much enjoyment is to be had in both creating and reading the coded

PLATE 75 △
The long, pale-green flower heads of greater plantain come to maturity piecemeal, a coronet of stamens gradually working their way downwards. Work the body of the flower head in a series of lozenge shapes (Fig 56) and then dot in a halo of tiny pink stamens, which lie over the other stitches to the front of the motif, and then disappear behind it.
Many wildflowers native to other countries, such as trillium, *have been imported into Britain, and sometimes hybridized, as garden plants*
23 x 15.5cm (9 x 6 inches)

messages in an embroidery. In Plate 75, the blue jay and *trillium* are native Canadians - where then is the link with Britain? The seed of the greater plantain *(Plantago major)* was introduced into North America on the shoes of the first settlers and was called 'Englishman's foot' by the American Indians because it seemed to flourish wherever Europeans trod (Fig 56). The golden maple leaves, of course, need no explanation – and their method of working, in common with the plantain, should present no problems by now.

And so to the Third World and subjects which are at once challenging, yet strangely familiar. The meerkats in Plate 76 *(Suricata suricata)* are, after all, only small furry animals – and we have had plenty of experience in those! They are not so very different from the stoat (Plate 58, page 97). Trees on the horizon may not have the profile of the English oak or Scots pine, but their outline can be embroidered in the same techniques, thorny scrub and low-growing herbs with the same basic stitches as the blackberry and common daisy.

Fig 56
'Englishman's foot'

PLATE 76 ▷
African meerkats stand ramrod straight in the heat of the desert, a landscape of strange, stunted scrub where large trees find survival difficult beneath a deep blue canopy, but small animals thrive in the relative coolness of the thorny undergrowth
Embroidery shown life size:
20.5 x 24cm (8 x 9½ inches)

An album is a 'blank book'. Only when it is filled does it become interesting, inspirational, thought provoking. The things which you choose to fill your album are entirely your decision – as is how and why. What is certain is that the countryside – whether close by and familiar or distant and strange – is changing year by year. Some scenes may disappear for ever, new ones will take their place. If your embroideries record the changes you will have a fascinating record in an extraordinary medium.

APPENDIX A

Basic Techniques

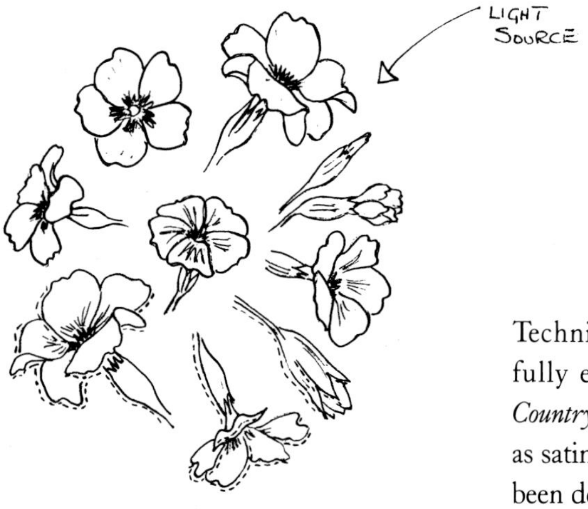

LIGHT SOURCE

Fig A1 △
The bottom three motifs show the shadow line if the light within *the picture comes from the top right*

Techniques explained here are more fully explored in *The Embroiderer's Countryside*. Conventional stitches, such as satin stitch, stem stitch, etc, have not been described as they may be found in any good embroidery textbook.

outlining and voiding

These two techniques define and differentiate between planes of stitching.

Outlining – also referred to as shadow lining. Only used in work on a pale background. Imagine where the light is coming from *inside* your picture and work a fine line of stem stitch, in black, along the opposite edge of each motif (see Fig A1).

Voiding. Used in work on pale or black background. Where one element of a design overlaps another, leave a narrow line 'void' of stitching. The line should be approximately the width of the gauge of thread used.

radial stitching

Close ranks of stitching apparently emanating from a single core and describing a wedge, arc or full circle. Stitches are taken from the outside of the motif inwards, where necessary disappearing behind their neighbours. Two or more 'strata' of radial stitching are necessary to build up a broad motif (see Figs A2 and A3).

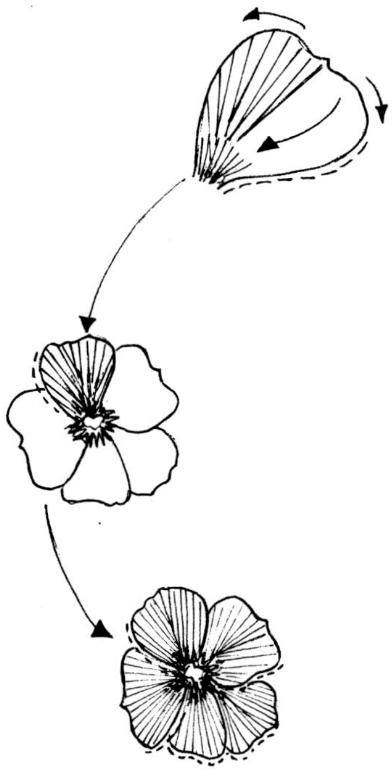

Fig A2 △
Radial lines shown suggest only about one in four of the stitches needed to complete each motif

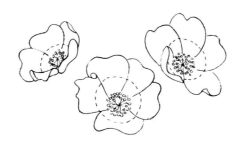

Fig A3 △
A second stratum of radial stitching should begin at approximately the level of the dotted line, blending smoothly into the first

Fig A4 △
Radial strata roughly equate to the markings on the bird's head – the eye should always be worked at an opposite angle to the main body of the opus plumarium

opus plumarium

Literally 'feather work'. Following the principle of radial stitching, as many strata as necessary blend together to fill large areas (see Fig A4).

Dalmatian-dog technique

The method of incorporating features within *opus plumarium* to form a single smooth plane: ie work black spots and then embroider a white dog around them. Ensure that the elements to be included are worked at the same angle of stitching as the embroidery which is to surround them. Blend together smoothly without outline or voiding.

opposite angle embroidery

Used where a motif reflexes, eg on a leaf or petal. The reverse of the subject should be worked at the same, but opposite, angle as the existing radial *opus plumarium* (see Fig A5).

snake stitch

Used to fill a field too narrow for *opus plumarium* and too wide for stem stitch. Beginning at a centre of a motif, work satin stitch first towards one extremity and then the other in the direction as indicated in Fig A6.

ticking

Short stitches overlaying *opus plumarium* worked at exactly the same angle as the underlying work, but taken in the opposite direction. Often used to describe the fine markings on the heads and underparts of birds.

studding

Short stitches overlaying *opus plumarium* worked at the opposite angle to the underlying stitches. Used when scale does not permit the working of Dalmatian-dog technique, eg on the underside of small butterflies or in miniature work.

shooting stitch

Long straight stitches taken over radial work but in the opposite direction to the existing stitches. Often used to describe fine markings at the centre of flowers.

laddering

Technique to illustrate 'chequerboard' markings, fish scales, etc. Fill the field to be worked with satin stitch or, if necessary, radial work. Using a contrasting shade, weave backwards and forwards through the existing stitches (without going through the background fabric), leaving the work fairly loose so that it can be 'pushed' into the correct position.

subdued voiding

Used to 'soften' outlines where a less definite demarcation zone between fields is required, eg on animals, birds, etc. Choose a colour which matches the

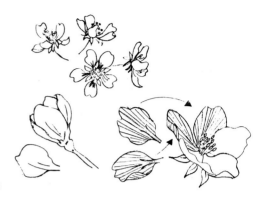

Fig A5 △
Even on small motifs the opposite angle principle is important. Where the underside of a petal comes into view, the angle of the stitching is reversed, as indicated by the hatching

Fig A6 △
Snake stitch. One direction is always from the centre to the tip of a motif, the other from the centre to the core

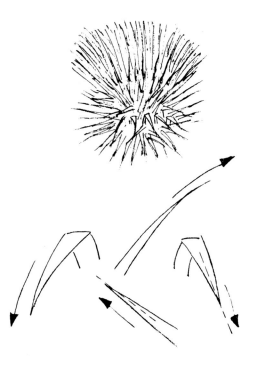

Fig A7 △
Remember that prickles often reflex. Where the underside is in view it should be embroidered in a darker shade. The single fine long stitch forming the spine is added after the rest of the work is complete

upper plane, and, at exactly the same angle, work straight stitches in a fine thread spanning the void.

straight stitching

Any technique which involves the use of either (1) single straight stitches to represent a whole motif, eg a single blade of grass, or (2) straight stitches worked in unison, but without imitating *opus plumarium*, eg distant grassland, water, sky, tree trunks, etc.

seed stitching

Worked directly on to the background fabric – not superimposed over other embroidery. Fine, very short, straight stitches. Often used as leaves on distant trees.

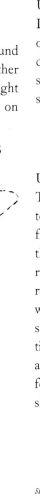

chevron stitch

Used to convey any straight prickle. Take two long straight stitches, angled to meet at the tip of the motif. Infill with a third straight stitch, if necessary. Using a finer thread, take a long straight stitch through the body of the spine, extending beyond the tip. Shadow line if worked on pale fabric (see Fig A7).

'straight' wings

Used for small insects in flight, eg bees. Do not transfer the outline of the wing on to the fabric. Referring to your design, work a radial series of fine, straight stitches allowing the fabric to show through. Never shadow line.

honeycomb stitch

Used for dragonfly's wings, etc. Transfer only the outline of the wing on to the fabric. Work fine radial stitches from the edge of the wing to the body of the insect. Lay a short stitch over two radial stitches at right angles and repeat, brickwork fashion (see Fig A8 where this has been exaggerated for the sake of clarity). As these stitches are tightened the radial stitches will gradually be pulled in opposite directions to form a honeycomb pattern. Never shadow line.

◁ *Fig A8*
Honeycomb stitch. The 'brick' stitches must slightly overlap the radial stitches so that when they are tightened, they will gently separate the underlying work to reveal the honeycombing

APPENDIX B

The Practicalities

working conditions and equipment

LIGHTING

Daylight is the finest and most natural light of all but if daylight is not available or not sufficient a good spotlight is a worthwhile investment.

Always work with the spotlight in the same position in relation to your embroidery, so that you become familiar with the angle of the light. Any shadow cast by your hand will soon become unnoticeable. Keep the light in such a position that any shadow will not cut across the stitching.

If you are working on a fine fabric, avoid having a high level of light immediately behind the work, as this will have the effect of making the fabric transparent, and can be very distracting. If you are working outdoors keep the sun behind you, but wear a hat or use a sun shade, as concentration plus sunlight can lead to headaches and eyestrain.

EMBROIDERY FRAMES

In fine flat embroidery the tension of the background fabric is all important and it is essential to work on an embroidery frame. Round 'tambour' frames,

◁ Fig B1
With the thumb on the outer ring of the tambour frame, the fingers of the hand should just be able to reach the centre of the circle. Similarly, with a larger frame, with the elbow at the ring, the fingers should reach the centre

so called because they resemble a tambourine, are best suited to fine work, as the tension they produce is entirely uniform. A free-standing frame is especially useful when techniques such as couching are to be included in the work, as these require two hands.

Tambour frames are available in a range of materials, but whichever frame is chosen it is essential that it should feel comfortable to use. If the diameter is more than approximately 35cm (14 inches) it can become too heavy, when dressed, to be hand held without making the arm tired, so it should therefore be free-standing. Ideally, a

Note: Much of the information contained in Appendix B is explained in greater detail in *The Embroiderer's Countryside*, pages 125–34.

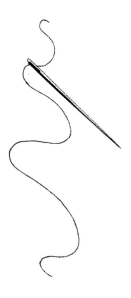

hand-held tambour frame should be small enough for the fingers of the hand in which it is held to reach from the outer rim to the centre of the frame without straining, as they will be able to guide the needle when it is on the reverse of the fabric. For free-standing frames, a good rule of thumb is that the embroiderer should be able to reach to the centre of the dressed frame without stretching unduly when the elbow is at the level of the outer rim.

OTHER EQUIPMENT

The choice of smaller tools is a personal one. Embroidery scissors must be small, fine and sharp, whatever their design. The finer your choice of threads, the sharper and keener the scissors must be.

Needles, too, must be chosen with the specific use of threads and fabric in mind. It is a good idea to have a selection of various sizes to avoid frustration when a new piece of work is begun. Sizes 5 to 10 are generally the most useful. For metallic threads use either a wide-eyed embroidery needle or a crewel needle of suitable size, depending on the technique.

If you use a thimble, be sure that it fits snugly and be careful that it has no worn or jagged edges which may catch in the work – this applies to all the tools discussed.

materials

There are no 'right' or 'wrong' choices when it comes to choosing fabric and thread so long as certain practical considerations are borne in mind. For so-called flat-work embroidery which must be worked in a frame, it is essential that the fabric chosen for the background does not stretch. If it stretches even slightly while embroidery is in progress, when removed from the frame it will contract to its normal size, and the embroidery will be distorted.

Larger pictures should be worked on heavier fabrics, smaller studies on light-weights, but this rule can be adapted to the particular needs of the picture in question.

Try to avoid fabrics with too loose a weave, as too many stitches will be vying for space in too few threads of warp and weft and the result will be unsatisfactory. Pure cotton and linen evenweaves are also ideal, but as a general rule for this type of 'freestyle' embroidery, if the weave is open enough to be used for counted thread embroidery it is too wide for us!

The choice of threads depends upon a number of factors. Stranded cottons are adaptable and widely available in a large range of colours. When split down into single threads they can be delicate enough to convey all but the finest details, and are fine enough to allow themselves to be 'mixed' in the needle. Avoid those skeins which vary their shades throughout their length, they are rarely convincing. It is better to re-thread your needle several times with slightly different shades. Shiny rayons and nylons can also be attractive, but their colours may not be as natural as you could wish, so choose carefully.

Pure silk threads are, of course, the finest and most enjoyable to use, though their behaviour in the needle can be frustrating to beginners. There are many different types of silk thread to choose from. 'Floss' silks are untwisted and therefore very shiny. The advantage of using floss is that it can be split down into very fine strands for the minutest detailed work, and then used doubled, or even trebled, to describe the more substantial parts of the design. For this reason it is ideal when it comes to 'mixing' colours in the needle. An almost infinite variety of shades can be achieved, which is particularly important for natural history subjects. The disadvantages of floss is that by virtue of its untwisted state it can fragment in the needle during the course of working, and especially if you have rough skin, can catch, fray and generally become very irritating! One solution to this problem is to make sure that your hands remain as smooth and soft as possible, and remember that a rough fingernail (or any other jagged edge) can damage your work almost beyond repair if it catches in embroidery already in situ.

Twisted silks are slightly easier to work with and also have a glorious shine. If they are not twisted too tightly, they may be split down into finer strands for detailed work, and then used in their original state for covering large areas. They are also useful in combination with floss silks to describe areas which do not require such a high level of sheen, for instance, buildings, roads and other man-made aspects of country life.

Stranded silks are a fairly recent innovation. These are a great boon to anyone used to stranded cottons, as they are in similar format and may be used either split into single threads or as up to six strands together. They are flexible, easy to use, come in a delightful range of colours and are altogether

recommended as having the best elements of both floss and twisted silk.

Initially you will need to buy a range of universally useful colours which will adapt themselves to your preferred subject matter. Decide upon about six basics and get up to three shades of each. For instance, green is obviously a prerequisite of any countryside embroidery project, so buy a true mid-toned green, together with a paler version of the same colour and a darker one for shadowing, etc. Similarly with browns, pinks, blues, yellow/orange and lilac. Needless to say, white and black are also essentials.

The choice of metallic thread is wide and varied; plan an excursion to a good needlework shop and have fun choosing for yourself!

Finally, of course, there are all the little extras which make collecting threads and materials more than a practical job and take it into the realms of fantasy. Specialist threads, tiny seed pearls and beads, and the occasional sequin and feather all deserve a place in some secret little glory-hole at the back of your workbox.

twisting floss silk

As you become more advanced in your designs you may find that you wish to mix several types of thread in a single picture – for instance a pure silk embroidery may need to incorporate a number of different textures in the same colours. Silk is expensive and if you have built up a palette of basic colours in floss, it is possible to double your range of effects by learning the simple technique of plying or twisting, thus

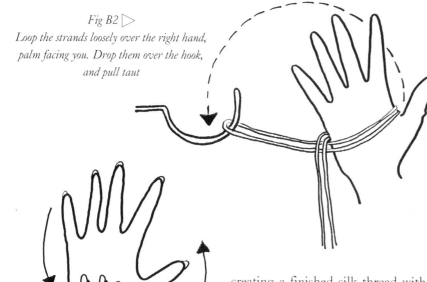

*Loop the strands loosely over the right hand,
palm facing you. Drop them over the hook,
and pull taut*

Fig B3 △

*Holding the strand(s) firmly against the heel of
the right hand, roll them upwards with the
fingertips of the left. Bringing the left hand
downwards at the same rate helps to create a
smoother thread*

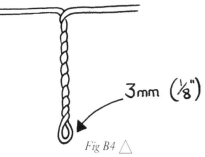

3mm (⅛")

Fig B4 △

*Scale x2 approx. Releasing the tension allows
the thread to twist on to itself. If the correct
tension has been achieved it should do so
smoothly, form the appropriate loop and
disentangle itself easily when pulled straight*

creating a finished silk thread with a matt lustre rather than a high gloss.

When using several strands of silk together in the needle to create a single thread (such as when mixing colours), the single thread created is referred to as being *two into one* (written 2/1) or *three into one* (3/1) and so on depending upon how many strands are being used. This may be followed by 'F' or 'T' to denote either free or twisted. The most easily created twists are 2/1T and 4/1T. When practising the technique it is best to use fairly thick strands; finer gauges can be used later. You will need something around which to loop your thread as you twist. If possible, find an inconspicuous spot where you can screw in a cup-hook and leave it for future use. Whatever you use it must be unmoving and thin. To create a 2/1T:

1 Cut a length of floss about 90cm (3 feet) long.

2 Catch it around the hook and even up the ends. Holding both ends in your left hand, create a loop with your right hand and drop the loop over the hook.

Move one strand around the hook so that a single strand is coming from each side.

3 Take the strand coming from the right of the hook and hold it against the heel of the right hand with the fingertips of the left. Roll the strand up the right hand, catch it at the fingertips and repeat.

4 Release the tension on about a third of the strand. The loop formed should be about 3mm (⅛ inch) across.

5 Pull the twisted strand to one side and tape it to a firm object to prevent it from unwinding. Repeat steps 3 and 4 above with the other strand, twisting it in the same direction. You have now *undertwisted* your thread.

6 Bringing the two twisted strands together, make the first motion of a simple knot, by passing one end over the other. Hold the ends of both strands against the heel of the left hand with the right fingertips and roll the strands up the left hand. Check the tension by repeating 4 above, but this time the reverse twist should mean that the thread will not form a loop. If the ply is too loose (ie the thread is not holding together) apply a further reverse twist. The thread is now *overtwisted* and ready to use.

To create a 4/1T the same procedure is followed, substituting a pair of strands on either side of the hook for the single strand used in a 2/1T.

For a 3/1T it is necessary to split one of the single strands in half in order that you can twist one and a half strands on either side of the hook.

using blending filaments

Blending filaments (fine specialist threads containing cellophane or metallic strands) are intended to be used in conjunction with other threads to highlight and emphasize features. They can either be used loosely in a 2/1F thread, making up half the thickness of the thread, more subtly as a smaller percentage of a 3/1F or 4/1F, or twisted into a 2/1T, 3/1T or 4/1T, making a much more compact thread. To use them in twisted threads, follow the procedures set out above, substituting the blending filament for as many strands of the finished thread as you require.

They may also be split down into their essential elements, giving the opportunity of including a fine cellophane strand alone with floss silk, or twisted into a very narrow 2/1T.

translating your sketches

Whether you are working from your own sketch, from a design suggested by the drawings in this book, or from a photograph or pre-prepared design, the first step is to transfer the pattern from paper to fabric. It is important to remember that every line which is transferred on to your background fabric is there permanently, and must therefore be covered by embroidery. Very fine details should be omitted from the transfer process, as fine embroidery would not be heavy enough to disguise the transferred line. Such fine detail must be worked freehand at a later date.

For transferring a design to fabric you will need:
- Tracing paper
- A large piece of firm cardboard (or wooden drawing board)
- Straight pins (drawing pins)
- Dull pencil, or other stylus
- Ruler
- Dressmaker's carbon paper (dressmaker's tracing paper)
- A flat, smooth table
- Background fabric (remember to leave a large border around your work for mounting).

Tracing paper is available in various weights. A good weight is approximately 90gsm, but you may need to undertake a little trial and error before you find the right weight for your chosen fabric.

DO NOT be tempted to use a typewriter carbon paper. The carbon will rub off on the fabric and is very difficult to remove. Dressmaker's carbon paper (or dressmaker's tracing paper) which is available in most fabric and embroidery stores and haberdashery departments

Fig B5 ▽
When planning your design, you may like to use the classical 'perfect dimension' of 16:9, on which the Parthenon was based. Seen empty, the resulting rectangle seems elongated, but the dimension becomes easily filled and is strangely harmonious to the human eye. It can be used landscape or portrait

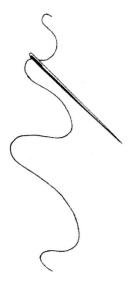

is designed specifically for our purposes. It is usually to be bought in packets of assorted colours and has a hard, waxy finish.

METHOD

1 Make a tracing of the chosen design. Place a sheet of tracing paper (this may have to be cut to size) over the pattern and carefully draw over each line with a lead pencil. In any large areas of the design which will be entirely covered by embroidery, you may wish to indicate the direction of stitching by shading. Check that you have traced all the required information (minus fine detail) before removing the paper from the design.

2 Place the cardboard on a flat surface, and lay your fabric out on it. If you use a wooden drawing board make sure that it is padded with several sheets of lining paper as this is necessary to produce a smooth, even line. Carefully position the traced design over the fabric, making sure that the 'north/south' alignment of the design is in line with the weave of the fabric. If the design is to be centred, use a ruler to find the midpoint. Pin the design to the fabric and into the board at the four corners, using the drawing pins.

Do not forget the importance of leaving a good sized border around your work, for effect as well as mounting. Your design may suddenly look very small on a large expanse of fabric, but this is only an illusion.

3 Choose a sheet of carbon paper in a colour which contrasts to your fabric. (White 'chalked' carbon paper will rub off as work progresses, so beginners may prefer to use the more waxy yellow or orange carbon paper on dark fabrics.)

Slip the carbon, colour side down, between the tracing and the fabric, removing one of the corner pins to do so. Replace the pin. Do not pin through the carbon paper. Using your pencil (your pencil should be dull, as a sharp pencil applying a hard pressure to the tracing paper will damage it) trace a few lines of the design. Remove one of the pins, raise one corner of the tracing and the carbon and check the impression. If the result is too heavy, apply slightly less pressure, if it is too light, a little more pressure. Replace the sheets and the pin and trace the whole of the design through on to the fabric. Take care not to smudge the carbon by resting your hand on top of the tracing while

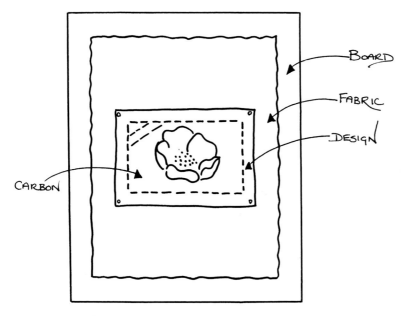

Fig B6 △
The carbon paper, shown partly hatched, is interleaved carefully between the background fabric and the design paper

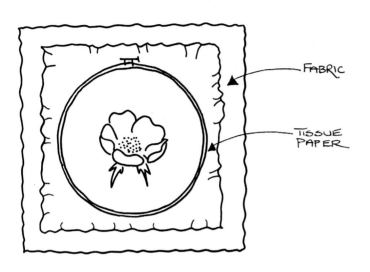

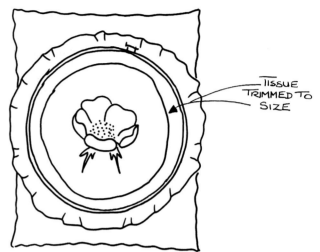

working, and do not let the pencil mark the fabric.

4 Remove the carbon and all but two of the top pins and check that all the design is transferred before removing the tracing.

PREPARING THE EMBROIDERY
There are various methods of 'dressing' a tambour frame. The procedure set out below has the advantage of not adding any weight to a hand-held frame and it may be used on all types and sizes of tambour frames.

1 Lay the inner ring of the tambour on a flat, clean surface.

2 Over this, place a sheet of tissue paper. If a large frame is used (ie larger than the individual sheets of paper) cut the tissue into wide strips and stick them loosely to the ring using double-sided sticky tape.

3 Position the fabric over this, and put a second sheet of tissue paper over both. If a large frame is used, cut wide strips

of the paper and lay them around the edges of the work.

4 Position the outer ring of the frame over the whole ensemble and press down smoothly but firmly. If using a keyed frame, tighten the screw to the appropriate tension.

5 Cut away the tissue paper to reveal the design beneath. Turn the frame over and cut away the tissue paper at the back to reveal the underside of the work. The remaining paper will protect the edges and avoid leaving a 'ring' around your finished work.

WORKING LARGE CANVASES
From time to time you may wish to work an embroidery which is too large to fit even a free-standing quilter's tambour frame. This was the case with the embroideries featured in Plate 8 on page 15 and Plate 44 on page 79. Special procedures must be followed in these cases, and great care taken that in moving the embroidery within the frame no damage is caused to the embroidery already completed, and no

Fig B7 (above left)
The tissue paper lies on top of the fabric, the upper ring of the frame ready to hold the two together. The design would be hidden beneath the tissue at this stage; it is shown here to indicate its position within the frame

Fig B8 (above right)
Once mated with its lower counterpart, the frame becomes whole, sandwiching two layers of tissue and fabric. The tissue is then cut away top and bottom to reveal the design, and conveniently trimmed around the outside of the ring for ease of handling

Fig B9 ▽
Cartoon for Plate 44. The work itself
62 x 26cm (24½ x 10 inches) is to be mounted
on a backing board of 72 x 36cm
(28½ x 14 inches), indicated by the outer line.
Enough fabric must also be allowed for folding
under and turning back (see Figs B13 and
B14). Worked on a free-standing tambour
frame 56cm (22 inches across), it is important
that the 'cut off' line (shown broken) should
pass through an area containing as little
activity
as possible, allowing the two areas to be
worked independently and merged as smoothly
as possible

smudges created in the transferred design. Using the cartoon for Plate 44 as an example (Fig B9), it is clear that only approximately half the design will comfortably fit the frame at any one time.

1 Decide which section of the embroidery you wish to work first. (If you are right handed this will be the left-hand section and vice versa.) Cover the inner ring of the frame with tissue paper as described above and lay the appropriate section of the fabric in position.

2 Place a second sheet of tissue paper over the fabric (as above) but where the transferred design is to be held between the rings of the frame place an extra couple of sheets as added padding.

3 Position the outer ring with the key (if any) at the top, press down and tighten as before.

4 Cut away the excess tissue paper to reveal the section to be worked (similarly on the reverse).

5 Pin a large sheet of tissue paper to the fabric, extending sideways to protect the design still outside the frame. Roll up the fabric with the tissue paper inside to protect the transfer and tape it to the edge of the frame.

6 When the first section of the embroidery has been completed, dismantle the frame and repeat the procedure above. Take particular care when assembling the rings positioned over embroidery

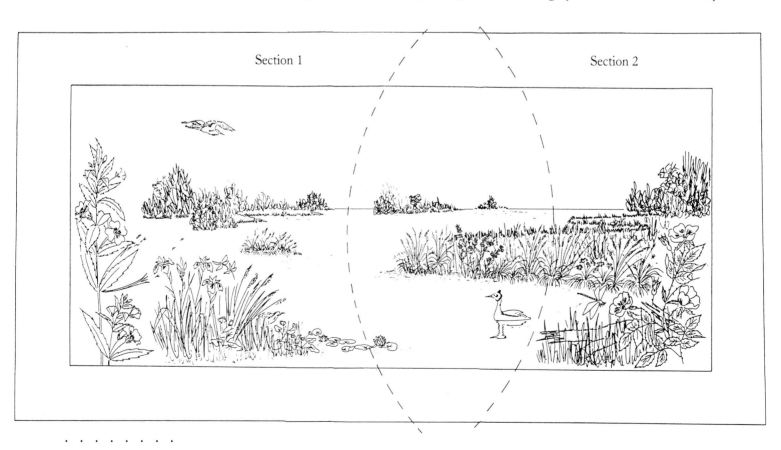

Section 1   Section 2

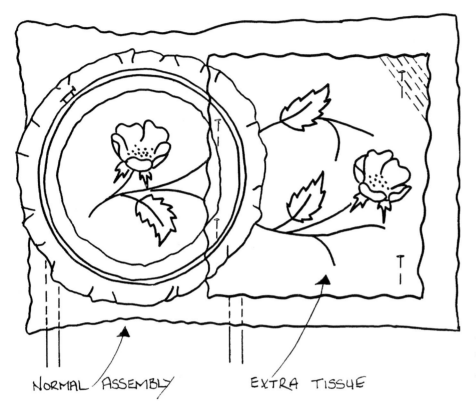

NORMAL ASSEMBLY   EXTRA TISSUE

◁ *Fig B10*
If possible, lay even a free-standing frame flat to achieve this assembly. The additional tissue paper, shown partly hatched is pinned loosely over the section of the design to be protected

already worked, and at stage 5 use several sheets of tissue paper to pad out and protect the fabric to be rolled up as this time it will include the embroidery itself!

WORKING A PAIR OF EMBROIDERIES

It is possible to economize on fabric, while still enjoying the flexibility of a free-standing frame, by working a pair of small embroideries at the same time on one frame. During the transfer process position the designs as shown in Fig B12. If you are left handed they will be mirrored. Make sure that you leave enough room between the two for them to be separated when work is complete and remember this must allow for the border around the work necessary for

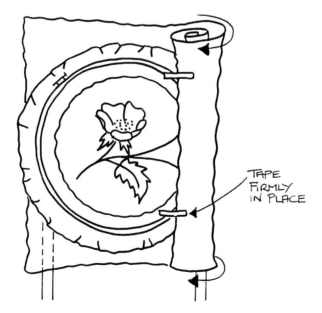

TAPE
FIRMLY
IN PLACE

Fig B11 △
A 'Swiss roll' of fabric and tissue paper is created and taped to the frame

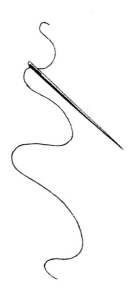

Fig B12 ▽
*If two embroideries are to be worked on a
single frame, remember to allow enough fabric
between the pair for mounting*

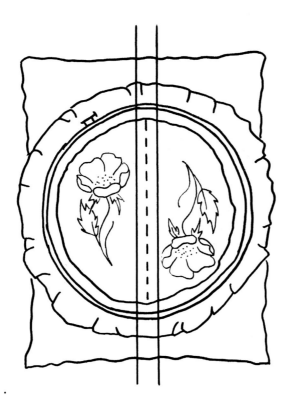

mounting etc. Position the key (if any) away from either of the designs.

At all times when not in use your frame and its precious contents should be covered and kept clean. Work on pale fabric, in particular, is vulnerable to the least speck of dirt. Always wash your hands before beginning to embroider and throw a cover over your frame if you leave it unattended – particularly if you are working outdoors!

presentation

MOUNTING
For mounting, you will need:
- Hardboard (or very stiff cardboard) cut to the size of the finished work (remember to make this big enough for the framing, and smooth off the edges thoroughly)
- Acid-free cartridge paper cut to the same size, white for work on a pale ground, black for work on black
- Clear sticky tape
- Fabric scissors
- Two large-eyed needles
- Lacing thread (mercerized cotton, or similar thread which will not stretch)
- Iron and ironing board.

METHOD
1 Press the embroidery on the wrong side, without steam (after checking the manufacturer's instructions for fabric and thread).

2 Using a small amount of sticky tape, secure the cartridge paper to the surface of the board.

3 Position the embroidery right side up over the covered board, and leaving a margin of at least 4cm (1½inches) cut the fabric to size. Leave a larger margin for larger pieces of work or for heavy fabric.

4 Carefully, and without shifting the position of the embroidery in relation to the board, turn the whole ensemble over so that the embroidery is face down, with the board on top of it. Make sure you are working on a clean surface.

5 Cut a long but manageable piece of lacing thread, and thread a needle at each end of the thread, with two 'tails' of similar length.

6 Fold the two sides of the fabric to the centre of the board.

7 Working from the top, insert a needle on either side and lace the two sides of

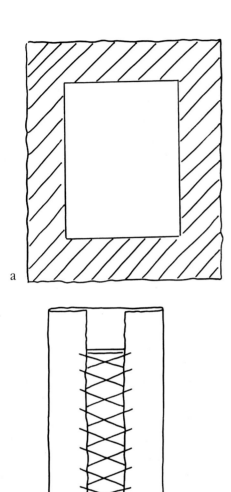

a

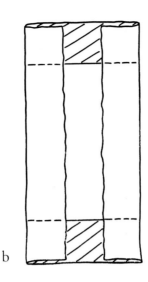

b

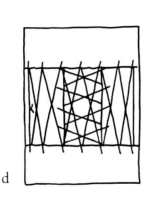

c

d

◁ *Fig B13*
Mounting the embroidery:
(a) Embroidery is placed face down, backing
board positioned on top
(b) The outer sides of the fabric are folded in
(c) They are laced, corset fashion
(d) The top and bottom edges of the fabric are
treated similarly

the fabric together corset fashion until you reach the bottom. If you run out of lacing thread, simply tie the thread off and begin again with more thread.

8 Fold the top and bottom of the fabric towards the centre and repeat the lacing process. It takes a little practice to achieve perfect tension. Do not over-tighten the laces as they may break, or rip the fabric, but do not be afraid of creating a reasonable pull on the work as only in this way will the original tension of the fabric on the tambour be re-created. Always tie off the ends of the lacing thread with firm, non-slip knots, and snip off any extra thread which is left.

MOUNTING LARGE EMBROIDERIES
Particular care must be taken when preparing a large embroidery for mounting. The larger the canvas, the greater the tension which may be needed to keep it taut on its backing board. Before lacing, therefore, the edges of the work should be turned back to allow the lacing thread to pass

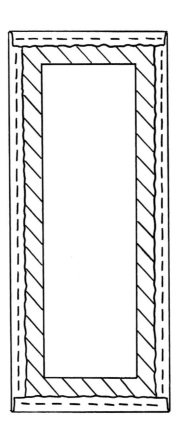

Fig B14 ▷

With the embroidery face down and the board in position, turn back a 'hem' of fabric and tack in position. When lacing the work in place stitch through both layers of the hem for added strength when mounting a large or oddly proportioned piece

6 Work a line of running stitch approximately 3 or 4 cm (1–1½ inches) inside the edge of the fabric, leaving the ends of the lacing thread on the right side of the embroidery.

7 Check that the design is still centrally located and draw up the running stitches. Tie off the thread and snip off the excess.

8 The pleats of fabric which have been formed by drawing up the lacing thread will be standing proud. Using an iron at the correct temperature press them firmly all in one direction.

MINIATURES

The basic process for mounting miniatures is similar to that described above for either straight-edged, circular or oval work. However, remember that your frame will be a great deal smaller, not only in width and height, but also in depth (ie rebate; see 'Framing' below). The margin of fabric to be turned back, while wide enough to safely accept the lacing thread, should be as narrow as possible to avoid bulk; similarly the lacing thread itself. It should not be necessary to exert great tension on a very small piece, as the embroidery itself will be very light.

It is particularly important to check that there are no specks of dust, fluff or tiny pieces of silk adhering to the front of a miniature before framing. Something the size of a pinhead which might be overlooked on a larger piece, will assume major proportions on a study only 2 inches high. It is a good idea always to make a careful inspection of the front of the work, whatever its

through two thicknesses of fabric. When put under pressure the fabric will be less likely to tear.

When mounting a long, narrow embroidery (such as that featured in Fig B9) lace whichever dimension is the greater first. Do not pull the lacing too tight, as even a rigid backing board, such as hardboard, will bow if put under excessive tension.

CIRCULAR OR OVAL MOUNTS

Repeat sections 1 to 4 under 'Method' on page 138, but leave a slightly larger border of fabric around the backing board.

5 Cut a piece of lacing thread the length of the circumference of the circle of fabric and thread a single large-eyed needle.

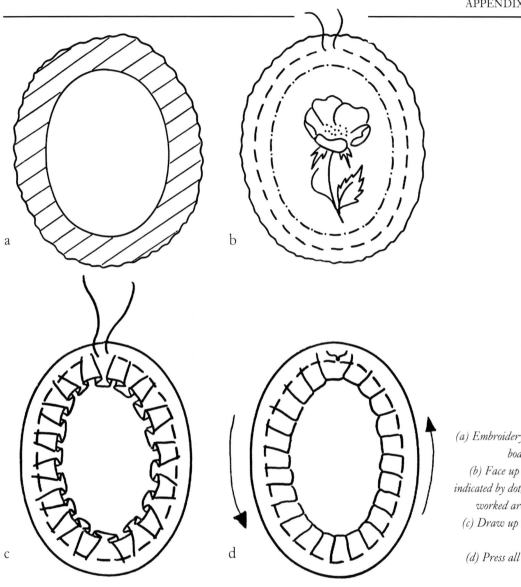

◁ *Fig B15*
(a) Embroidery face down, the oval mounting board is placed on top
(b) Face up (position of mounting board indicated by dot/dash line) running stitches are worked around the edge of the fabric
(c) Draw up the running stitches to form a series of pleats
(d) Press all the pleats in one direction to reduce bulk

size, before moving on to the final stage of presentation.

FRAMING
The choice of frame is a personal matter, but always be prepared to take professional advice, as framing can make or mar a picture. On a practical level, the rebate on any frame must be deep enough to accommodate the mounted work, the window mount required to lift the glass from the work (essential if beads etc have been used), the glass and a sheet of cardboard holding the ensemble together.

Avoid hanging work immediately above radiators or fireplaces, and avoid bathrooms and kitchens. No picture should be hung in direct prolonged sunlight. However, to be seen to their best advantage, embroideries need a good level of lighting and ordinary daylight will do little harm. A small spotlight positioned so that it illuminates the work from above will bring it to life, especially in the evenings. Take a little time to achieve the most effective angle of lighting.

BIBLIOGRAPHY

Anon, *Beowulf* Anglo Saxon Poetry (Everyman, 1926)

Carroll, Lewis, *Alice in Wonderland* (Grosset and Dunlap Inc, 1946)

Dickens, Charles, *David Copperfield* (Oldhams Press, *c*.1950)

Fitzgerald, F. Scott, *The Great Gatsby* (Penguin Books, 1950)

Grahame, Kenneth, *The Wind in the Willows* (Methuen & Co, 1959)

Kingsley, Charles, *The Water Babies* (Everyman, 1908)

Kipling, Rudyard, *Something of Myself* (Macmillan & Co, 1937)

Lee, Laurie, *Cider with Rosie* (Hogarth Press, 1959)

Noyes, Alfred, 'The Highwayman' *The School Book of English Verse* (Macmillan & Co, 1938)

Orwell, George, *Nineteen Eighty-Four* (Martin Secker and Warburg, 1949)

Stevens, Helen M., *The Embroiderer's Countryside* (David & Charles, 1992)

Tolkein, J.R.R., *The Fellowship of the Ring* (George Allen and Unwin, 1954)

ACKNOWLEDGEMENTS

Saying thank you to all those who offered help and encouragement in the preparation of this book hardly seems enough. To my husband (who broke me into the joys of word processing) and my parents – I can only wonder at your patience! To professionals – many thanks again for your expertise and unfailing enthusiasm – Nigel Salmon and his team, Angela Salmon and Sheila Haman (photographers extraordinaire), Vivienne Wells and the PR team!

Lastly to all my clients who kindly agreed to have their pictures reproduced in this book. Without you it would be a great deal shorter . . .

Plate 2, Miss H. L. Poole; 6, Mrs J. Allen; 7, Mrs Sheila Mills; 8, 16, 22, The House of Commons Works of Art Committee; 10, Mr and Mrs J. Robinson; 11, 24, 55, 58, Mrs D. Anstead; 12, 13, 23, 57, Mr B. J. W. Miller; 17, Dr and Mrs John Eades; 18, Gill Murphy; 25, 26, Mrs A. F. Stevens; 27, Mr B. Rayner; 29, Marjorie Bumphrey; 30, 31, Michael and Elaine Church; 33, Mrs Ann Peel; 34, Mrs Elizabeth Plumb; 35, Miss E. M. Claydon; 36, Judith Harman; 37, M. and T. Cannon; 38, Joan Hoare; 39, Mrs Sheila Wakerley; 40, 41, 43, Bonnie Adie; 42, Mrs E. G. Starling; 44, 45 Mrs J. Bruce; 46, Dr and Mrs B. J. Poole; 47, Mr and Mrs J. Deering; 52, Norah Salmon (Mr and Mrs G. E. Hutchinson); 53, Mrs June Baines; 54, Mrs M. E. Baker; 56, Mr and Mrs J. M. Bryant; 63, Jill Mitchinson; 65, Miss Lucy Sortwell; 66, Miss R. Hemmant; 67, Mr and Mrs R. Abraham; 73, Mrs A. Froggatt, 74, Dennis White (Mrs June Murdoch).

INDEX

. . . .